Decision Mc
EXERCISES
for GCSE Geography

Peter and Carole Goddard

Nelson

Thomas Nelson & Sons Ltd
Nelson House
Mayfield Road
Walton-on-Thames
Surrey KT12 5PL
United Kingdom

I(T)P® Thomas Nelson is an International Thomson Publishing Company

I(T)P® is used under licence

© Peter and Carole Goddard, 1998
Illustrations © Thomas Nelson & Sons Ltd 1998

First published by Thomas Nelson & Sons Ltd 1998

ISBN 0-17-434315-9
9 8 7 6 5 4 3 2 1
02 01 00 99 98

All rights reserved. No part of this publication may be reproduced, copied or transmitted in any form or by any means, electronic or mechanical, including photocopy, recording, or any information storage and retrieval system, without permission in writing from the publisher or under licence from the Copyright Licensing Authority Ltd., 90 Tottenham Court Road, London W1P 9HE.

Picture research: Image Select International Ltd
Design: Lorraine Inglis
Editorial: Linda Miles
Illustration: Gecko Ltd
Printed by Zrinski Printing and Publishing House, Čakovec, Croatia

Acknowledgements
The authors would like to thank the following organisations and acknowledge the following sources:

Chapter 1
The Australian Nature Conservation Agency, Kakadu National Park for Fig.1, p6; Fig. 6 (adapted), p8; material for the visitor guide display on p10; and Fig. 8, p11, all from or based on material in The Kakadu National Park Visitor Guide, 1988 and 1996. Particular thanks are also due to Energy Resources of Australia and The Bureau of Tourism Research.

Chapter 2
Fig. 2, p17: Map reproduced from the Ordnance Survey 1:10 000 scale mapping with the permission of The Controller of Her Majesty's Stationery Office © Crown copyright (399752), and with the permission of Manchester Airport plc and Scott, Wilson Kirkpatrick & Partners, Basingstoke.
Fig. 3, pp 18 and 19: Reproduced with permission from Manchester Airport plc.

Chapter 3
Fig. 2, p24, and Fig. 4, p26: Maps reproduced by permission of Geographers' A–Z Map Co Ltd and from the Ordnance Survey mapping with the permission of The Controller of Her Majesty's Stationery Office © Crown copyright (399752).
Fig. 6, p29: Mapping based on Ordnance Survey mapping with the permission of The Controller of Her Majesty's Stationery Office © Crown copyright 1997 (399752).
Overlay details originally published in a Report to the Acting Head of Planning to the Norwich City Council Planning Committee, 12 December 1996, and reproduced with permission.

Chapter 4
With thanks to Professor J. A. Allan, SOAS, University of London, for providing advice and access to resources.
Fig. 2, p34: Based on Atlas of Israel, Macmillan Publishing Company, New York, 3rd edn, 1985.
Fig. 3, p35: Climate statistics from the Israel Year Book and Almanac 1996, IBRT Translation/Documentation Ltd, Jerusalem.
Fig. 7, p37: Allan, J. A., personal communication.
Fig. 9, p38 and Fig. 11, p41: Allan, J. A., Water, Peace and the Middle East, Tauris Academic Studies, I.B., Tauris Publishers, London.
Fig. 10, p40: data: 1948–75: Lowi, Water and Power, Cambridge University Press, 1993; data: 1980–85: Israel Year Book and Almanac 1996.

Chapter 5
Fig. 3, p47: Map reproduced from the Ordnance Survey 1:25 000 scale mapping with the permission of The Controller of Her Majesty's Stationery Office © Crown copyright (399752).
Fig. 4, p49 and artwork, p53: Publicity material supplied by Bodiam Castle and reproduced with the permission of The National Trust, Lamberhurst.
Fig. 5, p50 and Fig. 6, p51: Kent and East Sussex Railway, Tenterden.

Chapter 6
Fig. 4, p57: Map reproduced with permission from Canterbury City Council, based on map reproduced from the Ordnance Survey mapping with the permission of The Controller of Her Majesty's Stationery Office © Crown copyright (399752), and with artwork taken from 'Rebuilding of Sea Defences, Central Parade, Herne Bay, Kent' prepared by Roberts, Beck and van Overeem.
Fig. 6, p59: Statistical data supplied by Canterbury City Council.
Figs 7, 8, 9 and 10, pp 60–63: Maps reproduced with permission from Canterbury City Council, based on maps reproduced from the Ordnance Survey mapping with the permission of The Controller of Her Majesty's Stationery Office © Crown copyright (399752), and from the Delft Hydraulics Report.
Fig. 11, p64: Map supplied by and reproduced with permission from Canterbury City Council, based on map reproduced from the Ordnance Survey mapping with the permission of The Controller of Her Majesty's Stationery Office © Crown copyright (399752).
Particular thanks are also due to the Chief Librarian at Herne Bay Library for research assistance, and to the staff at Canterbury City Council.

Chapter 7
Fig. 2, p68: Map reproduced from the Ordnance Survey 1:50 000 scale mapping with the permission of The Controller of Her Majesty's Stationery Office © Crown copyright (399752).
Fig. 6, p73: Based on diagram in Developing Wind Energy for the UK, M. Rand, Friends of the Earth, London, 1990.
Thanks are also due to Bond Pearce, solicitors, for their assistance.

Chapter 8
Maps and illustrations on pp 76, 80, 81, 82, 83, 84, 85 and 86: OS maps reproduced from the Ordnance Survey 1:25 000 scale mapping with the permission of The Controller of Her Majesty's Stationery Office © Crown copyright (399752); also with the permission of Terence O'Rourke plc, town planning consultants, Bournemouth, who produced 'Options for Ramsgate: Ramsgate Harbour Approach Road Route Evaluation' for Kent County Council, from which the maps and Fig. 6, p79, have been reproduced; and with the permission of Kent County Council.

Chapter 9
Fig. 3, p89 and Fig. 4, p90: Maps reproduced from the Ordnance Survey 1:50 000 scale mapping with the permission of The Controller of Her Majesty's Stationery Office © Crown copyright (399752), and for Fig 4: Source: 'Daventry District Local Plan – Statement of Decisions on the Inspectors' Recommendations and the List of Proposed Modifications', Daventry District Council, October, 1996.
Fig. 6, p93: Map reproduced from the Ordnance Survey 1:10 000 scale mapping with the permission of The Controller of Her Majesty's Stationery Office © Crown copyright (399752).

Chapter 10
Fig. 4, p100: Statistical data supplied by the Department of Transport from 'The A36 Salisbury bypass SACTRA assessment', August 1996, produced by Rendel, Palmer & Tritton, development and engineering consultants for the Highways Agency.
© Crown copyright is reproduced with the permission of The Controller of Her Majesty's Stationery Office. Fig. 8, p105 and pp 106, 107 and 108: Maps based on the Ordnance Survey mapping with the permission of The Controller of Her Majesty's Stationery Office © Crown copyright (399752).

Chapter 11
Fig. 6, p112: 'La Junta de Andalucia abre el camino para urbanizar el entorno de Doñana', Lola Yllescas, Quercus, Dec. 1996.
The authors would also like to acknowledge with thanks the assistance of Elena Lopez-Gunn at the University of Hertfordshire, the Tourist Office Almonte, and the Spanish National Tourist Office, London.

Chapter 12
Fig. 4, p119; Fig. 5, p120 and Fig. 10, p125: based on maps, illustrations and historical data in 'Phase III Option and Appraisal Report', Binnie, Black and Veatch, July 1996, The Environment Agency, Worthing. Fig. 8, p122: Geographical, May, 1994: based on map reproduced from the Ordnance Survey mapping with the permission of The Controller of Her Majesty's Stationery Office © Crown copyright (399752)

OS symbols, p128: Reproduced with the permission of The Controller of Her Majesty's Stationery Office © Crown copyright (399752).

Picture acknowledgements
Aerofilms: 25, 99   Colorific: 37, 44
Cumbria Picture Library: 69t, 74   Holt Studios:114
Index: 113   Kent Messenger: 56, 57   Manchester Airport: 18, 19, 20, 21, 22, National Wind Power: 69b   Photoair: 46, 77   Oxford Scientific Films: 7 bottom l&r, 112 l&r   Planet Earth Pictures: 7t, 10,   Still Pictures: 72   Trip: 13, 27, 30, 32, 36, 41, 91, 94, 95, 96, 102, 103, 104. Other photos supplied by the authors.

Every effort has been made to contact all copyright holders, but if any have been inadvertently overlooked, the publisher will be pleased to make the necessary arrangements at the first opportunity.

Decision Making EXERCISES *for* GCSE Geography

Peter and Carole Goddard

Nelson

Contents

1. Kakadu: conflicts in park management

2. A second runway for Manchester Airport?

3. How should Riverside be redeveloped?

4. Water management in Israel

5. Bodiam Castle

6. Replacing sea defences in Herne Bay

7. Should permission be given for a wind farm on Gunson Height?

8. Improving the approach road to Ramsgate Harbour (Port Ramsgate)

9. The development of Whitehills, Northampton

10. Salisbury bypass

11. Saving wetlands in Doñana

12. Flood alleviation in the Lavant Valley, Chichester

Kakadu: conflicts in park management

Background information

Figure 1 Location of Kakadu National Park and distances from main cities

Kakadu in the Top End of the Northern Territory (Fig. 1) is the largest and best known of Australia's parks. The scenic attractions of the area together with its scientific and recreational resources were recognised back in the 1950s, but because of conflicts between conservation, mining and Aboriginal interests the area was not declared a National Park until 1979. Even then, as Figure 2 shows, this status was awarded to only part of the park.

In the 1990s Kakadu, because of its diversity of landscapes, wealth of flora and fauna and its rich cultural heritage, was included in the World Heritage list. However, the conflicts are still major issues. How should these conflicts be resolved?

Environment

Figure 2 shows that the park area encompasses most of the drainage basin of the South Alligator River. The different types of scenery found in the park are shown on Figure 6. Each type supports a rich variety of flora and fauna adapted to the particular habitat. Kakadu experiences a tropical monsoon climate with marked wet and dry seasons. This rainfall pattern is reflected in the dramatic change in vegetation which alters the appearance of the landscape from season to season.

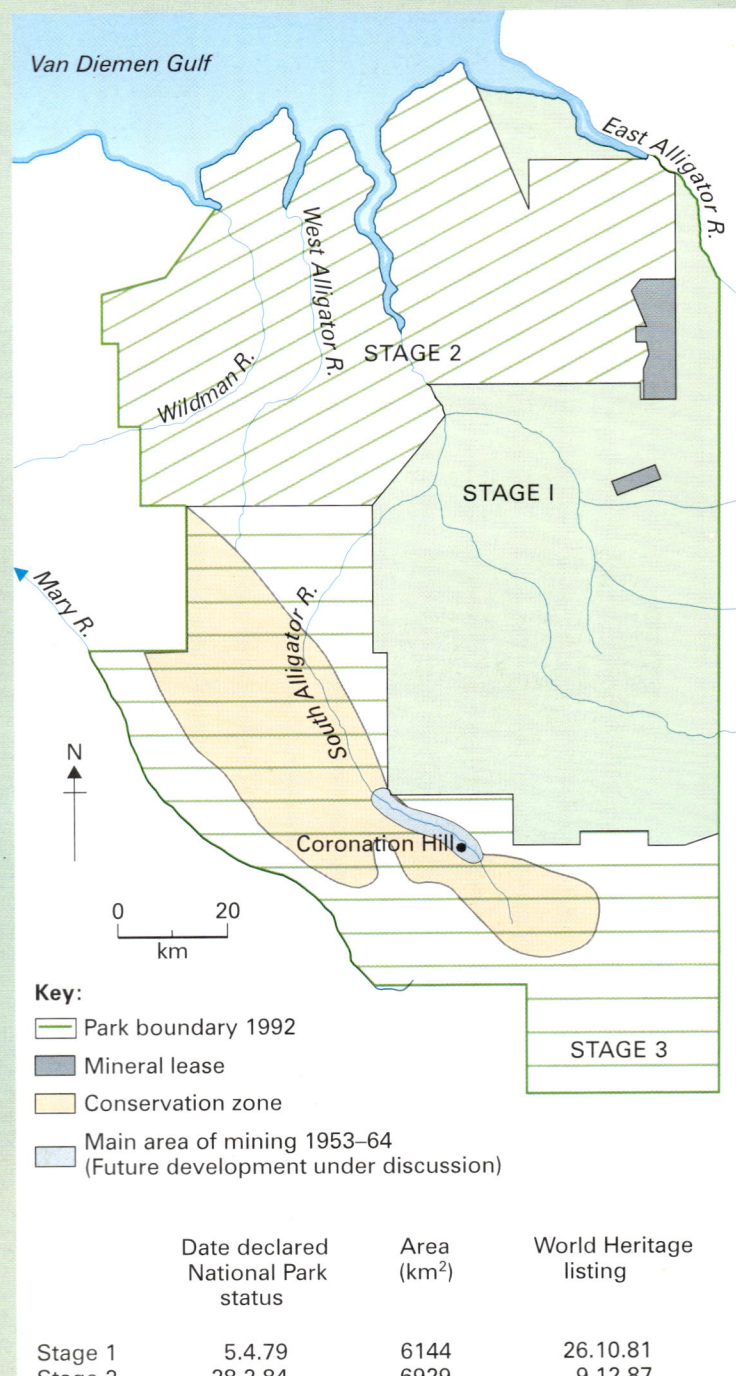

Key:
- Park boundary 1992
- Mineral lease
- Conservation zone
- Main area of mining 1953–64 (Future development under discussion)

	Date declared National Park status	Area (km²)	World Heritage listing
Stage 1	5.4.79	6144	26.10.81
Stage 2	28.2.84	6929	9.12.87
Stage 3 (excl. CZ)	12.6.87	2252	
Final stage 3	24.6.91		13.12.92
Total park		19 757	

Figure 2 Creation of Kakadu National Park

Escarpment and plateau

- the sandstone escarpment (Fig. 3) is the most spectacular feature of the park:
  - marks the edge of the Arnhem Land plateau
  - 200 m high in the south
  - waterfalls plunge over the edge in the wet season
- the plateau is criss-crossed by deep gorges and depressions
- monsoon rainforest is found in the gorges; shrubs and grasses occur on the plateau.

Undulating plains

- make up about half of the area
- open forest where eucalyptus predominate (Fig. 4) and grassland support a greater variety of plants and animals than any of the other physical divisions.

Figure 4 Open eucalyptus forest

Figure 3 Arnhem Land escarpment

Figure 5 Floodplains of the East Alligator River

Decision Making Exercises

Wetlands

- some of the world's most important tropical **wetlands**
- dramatic change in appearance between wet and dry seasons
- extensive floodplains or freshwater wetlands of the East and South Alligator Rivers are crossed by meandering streams in the dry season but are submerged in the wet season (Fig. 5)
- waterways are marked by paperbark trees (Fig. 7)
- important area for waterfowl
- important area for migratory birds.

Coastal mudflats

- mark seaward edge of the floodplains
- fringed with mangrove forest.

Southern hills (stone country)

- mainly in what was Stage III of the park
- mark transition between monsoon north and arid interior
- many rare or endangered plant and animal species.

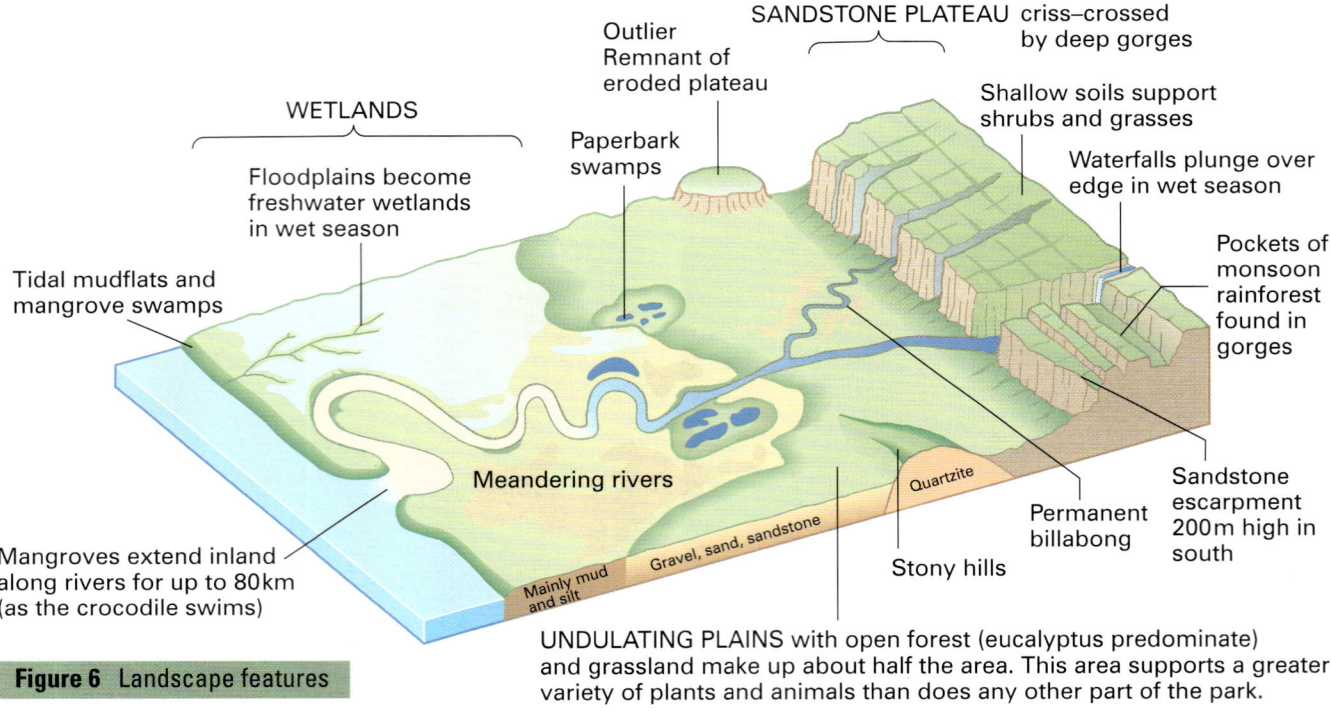

Figure 6 Landscape features

FOUNDATION

1. a) Which river system is almost entirely within the park?
   b) Name three other rivers.
2. The escarpment is the most striking feature of the landscape. Using Figures 3 and 6 describe the escarpment.
3. Using Figures 5 and 6 describe the wetlands in a) the dry season, b) the wet season.
4. Which landscape type occupies the largest area?
5. Suggest two reasons why Kakadu should be preserved in its natural state.

HIGHER

1. Explain fully why Kakadu was declared a National Park.
2. Using Figure 6, suggest why habitats vary from one region to another.
3. Why does the landscape vary in appearance from season to season?
4. Study Figure 6 carefully, then with the help of Figure 8 name a) an outlier, b) a waterfall, c) a river which meanders.
5. Sketch and label as many features shown in Figure 5 as possible.

The Aborigines

Much of Kakadu has been owned in common by the Aboriginal people since an Act was passed in 1976; in fact, the land is leased to Parks Australia.

> We Aboriginal people have inhabited this land for 50 000 years. We learned to live in harmony with the environment and moved about the land according to the seasons. We sought shelter at the foot of the escarpment or lived on the floodplain levees obtaining food from rivers and freshwater wetlands.

> The idea of tourism is not part of our heritage. We don't want to lose our rights and our culture.

> Conflict has occurred over mineral development at sacred sites, for example at Coronation Hill. It is important that our sacred sites are not disturbed.

> There are over 3500 Aboriginal sites. The best known are: Ubirr; Nourlangie; Nanguluwur. These sites have the largest and best-known collections of Australian rock art, but unfortunately they are being threatened by weather, termite nests and tourists.

> Now fewer than 300 Aboriginal people live in the park, scattered among 16 locations. We live a semi-nomadic life. We have maintained our bonds with the land and still observe our traditional beliefs and customs in the same way that our ancestors have done since the Dreamtime (Creation). We feel the park is our home and we must look after it. It provides up to 50 per cent of our diet. We help in park administration. Our traditional method of fire management led to good maintenance of the ecosystem, and it is still practised.

Decision Making Exercises

Tourism

Kakadu is a major tourist destination for both domestic and overseas visitors.

Read the tourist leaflet and work through the questions to find out why Kakadu attracts 33 per cent of all visitors to Northern Territory.

Visitor Guide

KAKADU NATIONAL PARK

Welcome to Kakadu!

Kakadu has much to offer you. Its name comes from the Gagudju Aboriginal language reflecting the important cultural heritage of the park. Visit the Aboriginal Cultural Centre near Yellow Water. Visit the archaeological sites used by the Aboriginal people for 60 000 years.

See the varied landscapes of the park and observe the variety of plants and animals. The Wetlands at Yellow Water are one of the most accessible places to see waterbirds and crocodiles.

Kakadu has

- 50 species of mammals
- 275 species of birds
- 75 species of reptiles
- 25 species of frogs
- 55 species of fish

Many species are rare or endangered.
Look at the map of the park (Fig. 8) to see the facilities we provide for our visitors.

Figure 7 Paperbark trees, Katherine River

Jabiru, large species of stork common to Kakadu

Kakadu: conflicts in park management

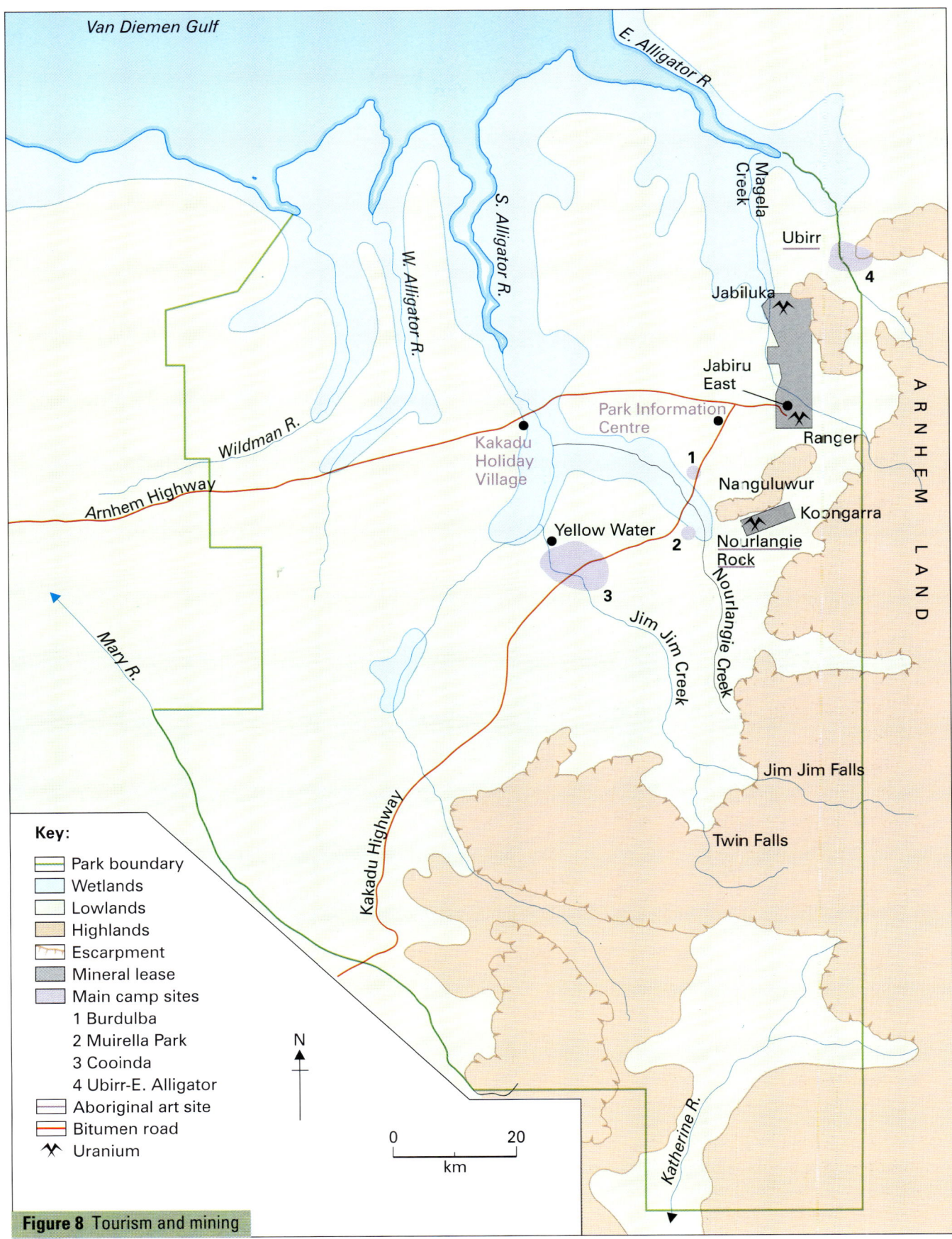

Figure 8 Tourism and mining

Decision Making Exercises

Kakadu: Tourism fact file

Tourist growth

| 1982 | 45 800 | 1986 | 130 000 | 1990 | 238 000 |
| 1985 | 100 000 | 1988 | 220 000 | 1995 | 235 000 |

Effects of tourist growth

Ecotourism is a fast-growing sector of Australia's tourist industry.

Effects of tourist growth on Kakadu
- Uncontrolled tourist growth may have substantial environmental impact, especially in 'honeypots' such as E. Alligator River, Ubirr, Nourlangie.
- Stricter controls have been introduced:
  - camp permits
  - closure of some long-established sites
  - new sites opened which preserve the environment but at same time satisfy visitors' requirements
  - fenced boardwalks at rock art sites.

Tourist season

Most visit in the 'dry' because:
- weather more pleasant
- most waterfalls can be reached only in 'dry'
- in 'wet' some roads and campsites may be closed.

Camping

75% of overnight private visitors and 30% of overnight tour visitors camp during part/all of stay.

FOUNDATION

1 Using information from Figure 6 and from the section on the Aboriginal people add to the list of attractions of Kakadu mentioned in the Visitor Guide. Group the attractions under the headings a) scenic, b) cultural.
2 Give three reasons why visitors prefer to visit in the 'dry'.
3 Write down three statements which show that tourism can be harmful to the park.
4 State two measures which are helping to reduce damage by tourism.

HIGHER

1 Explain fully why tourism threatens the environment.
2 What steps are being taken to lessen the effects of the adverse side of tourism?
3 Using information from the sections on the environment and the Aboriginal people, complete the Visitor Guide list of tourist attractions that Kakadu offers.

Kakadu: conflicts in park management

Mining

Kakadu is highly mineralised. Its deposits of uranium are important in the generation of nuclear power (i.e. electricity). The Ranger mine is the country's major uranium producer and supplies about 10 per cent of the Western world's uranium. It is an important export earner.

- In the late 1960s and early 1970s, major uranium deposits were discovered in Ranger and Koongarra, Narbalek and Jabiluka (Fig. 8). These areas have been excised from (not included in) the park.

- Ranger deposits are the only deposits at present worked. (Narbalek ceased operating in 1995.)
  - the project area is 78.6 km^2
  - the mining area is 4 km^2
  - production at Orebody No. 1 mine started in 1980; the mine was worked out in 1994
  - opencast mining made a pit 175 m deep, 750 m wide; 60 million tonnes of rock waste removed to obtain 18 million tonnes of ore; 5 million tonnes of rock waste used for the **tailings** dam and water storage ponds.

- Orebody No. 3 started production (opencast) in 1996 and is expected to continue until 2008.

- Ranger is one of the most environmentally regulated mines in the world:
  - the Environmental Division monitors water and air quality, and dust concentration
  - all rainfall run-off is collected in retention ponds and is carefully managed
  - land rehabilitation is an ongoing concern: each year a section of rock waste dump is revegetated; when operations finally cease, the site will be a low, rounded, tree-covered hill.

- Mining at Ranger employs about 230 people.

- Mining benefits tourism:
  - Energy Resources of Australia Ltd. (ERA) airstrip on the Ranger lease is a key tourist facility
  - extension of Arnhem Highway beyond S. Alligator River to Jabiru, constructed for Ranger is important road access
  - Jabiru provides facilities for tourists – hotel, banking, supermarket
  - ERA has contributed $126 million to tourism since 1982.

- Ranger has a good safety record but people fear that spills could occur.

Jabiluka may be opened up now that demand for uranium is growing and stockpiles are low.

- It is one of the richest uranium deposits in the world with 19.5 million tonnes of ore.

- There is an estimated 90 400 tonnes of uranium oxide, enough to generate 20 times Australia's current electricity needs.

- ERA would keep the environmental impact to a minimum.

- Mining at Jabiluka would benefit all Australians; with Ranger it would bring in $12 billion over the next 25 years; Aboriginal people would benefit from $210 million royalties.

- Jabiluka will employ 110 people.

Figure 9 Ranger mine

FOUNDATION

1. Look at Figure 9.
   a) Why is this mine unsightly?
   b) Why does it pose a threat to both vegetation and wildlife?
2. List the ways in which the mining company looks after the environment.
3. What are the benefits of mining uranium?

HIGHER

1. Why is mining a threat to the park although the mineral areas have been excised?
2. Why is it likely that another mine will be opened up?
3. Why do the Aboriginal people, tour operators and mining companies feel differently about the park and the way it is being developed?

Decision Making Exercises

The problem

Kakadu National Park has been the home of Aboriginal people for thousands of years. Since the 1950s modern commercial developments have threatened their lifestyle and the environment.

Tourism depends on the environment. Both tourism and mining earn large sums of money for Australia from which the Aboriginal people derive some benefit. Can these conflicts be resolved?

Assessment of the three options

Option 1 – Commercial development of Kakadu

- Mining in excised areas should be allowed to continue because uranium is important as an export earner and as an energy source.
- Mining provides **infrastructure** in remote areas, for example sealed (bitumen) roads such as Arnhem Highway, and telecommunications.
- Heavy rainfall in 'wet' causes problems with surplus water drainage and this poses a hazard to the environment.
- Mining companies claim that a) modern methods of exploitation cause minimal degradation of the environment, b) some areas are already degraded (in former Stage III of the park overgrazing by buffalo has occurred).
- Tourism provides jobs and local income.
- The park offers visitors scenic and recreational facilities and the opportunity to escape 'civilisation'.
- The growing number of tourists puts increasing pressure on the environment because of the need for more roads, hotels and camping facilities.
- New areas could be opened up to attract visitors away from 'honeypots'.
- Tourism intrudes on the privacy of Aboriginal people.
- Some Aboriginal people welcome visitors and see tourism as an opportunity to teach people about Aboriginal culture.
- Tourists damage rock art and do not always have respect for Aboriginal sacred sites.
- Tracks worn away by four-wheel drive vehicles lead to erosion.
- Camping areas suffer vegetation loss.
- In the wetlands boats cause pollution and disturb birdlife; overfishing occurs.
- If economic returns from tourism are large enough, there would be less need for more destructive economic activity (e.g. mining).

Option 2 – Conservation of Kakadu

- If no economic development is permitted, this would preserve a) the cultural heritage, b) flora and fauna – there are more than 1500 plant species.
- Conservationists wanted control of Stage III. Control of the headwaters of S. Alligator River are essential as contamination there would result in the destruction of the wetlands.
- Some damage has been caused by buffaloes (introduced in the nineteenth century) especially in the wetlands where they have broken down levees allowing saltwater to penetrate.
- Since Europeans settled in New South Wales 60 per cent of wetlands have been destroyed there.

Option 3 – Sustainable development

By careful park management it should be possible to balance the development of tourism and conservation. For the survival of the park it must be protected from the more destructive effects of tourism. Suggestions:
- limit numbers of tourists
- provide accommodation outside the park
- protect Aboriginal art
- educate visitors to take care of the park.

The Decision

FOUNDATION

1. What are the advantages of tourism in Kakadu?
2. a) What are the disadvantages of tourism?
   b) Put a tick by those you feel it would be possible to take protective measures against.
3. a) If you owned a mining company would you be more concerned about your profits or about possible harm to the environment?
   b) How could mining harm the environment?
4. If you were an Aboriginal would you feel that the commercial development of the park might benefit you in any way?
5. How might ornithologists and botanists feel about the park being developed commercially?
6. To help you decide which of the three options is best, follow the instructions below to make a matrix.
   a) Divide your page into three columns and head these: Commercial activity; Advantages; Disadvantages.
   b) Using your answers to questions 1 to 5 fill in the matrix grouping your facts, for example effects on the environment now and in the future; financial; job creation.

HIGHER

1. Selecting evidence from the whole study, give reasons in support of the option you think best.
2. For one of the other options, give reasons why it should not be adopted.

Summary

Kakadu was declared a National Park because of its variety and quality of landscape, wildlife and cultural heritage. Economic development threatens both the safety of the environment and the privacy of the Aboriginal people. It is important to preserve these natural and cultural features for the benefit of future generations. What is the way forward?

Glossary

ecotourism tourism promoting the appreciation and understanding of the natural and cultural environment

infrastructure power, communications, transport, etc. which are necessary for economic development

lease land on which the mining company has been granted permission to mine

sustainable development development that does not cause damage to the environment

tailings the fine slurry left after mining

wetlands shallow water environments temporarily or permanently flooded

2 A second runway for Manchester Airport?

Background information

The business community in the North West of England want an expansion of Manchester Airport so it can help to attract new industries to the region and so ease unemployment. The region would also greatly benefit in terms of employment because construction jobs would be created to build a new runway, in addition to the more permanent jobs in an expanded airport.

At the present time the existing single runway is operated at maximum capacity at peak times. At these peak times the airport handles 45 scheduled operations an hour, well beyond the capacity of other single runway airports in Europe. More airlines want to use Manchester but any not already based there are being turned away. Over 1 million passengers who live in the North West have to travel to Heathrow or Gatwick to start their journeys rather than starting them from Manchester, their local airport.

Noise and the second runway

- a guarantee has been given that noise levels will be lower with two runways than with one
- runway 2 will not normally be used at night
- current restrictions on night flying will continue
- older, noisier aircraft will be banned
- a target has been set for 96 per cent of all flights by the year 2000 to be the newest, quieter aircraft
- parked aircraft will use ground-based electrical supplies rather than having to run onboard engines
- more sound insulation will be provided for those living close to the airport.

Figure 1 Location of Manchester Airport

Manchester Airport fact file

- currently the third largest airport in the UK in terms of number of passengers (after Heathrow and Gatwick)
- one of the world's top 20 airports for the number of international passengers
- provides services to more than 175 long-haul and short-haul destinations in five continents
- provides services to 27 UK and Irish destinations
- provides a frequent shuttle service to both Heathrow and Gatwick
- fast transfer between domestic and international flights
- the first major world airport to provide 100 per cent baggage screening technology.

Passenger growth and forecast 1985–2005 (millions of passengers per year)

1985	1990	1993	1997	2000	2005
5	10	12	15	22	28

The runway plan

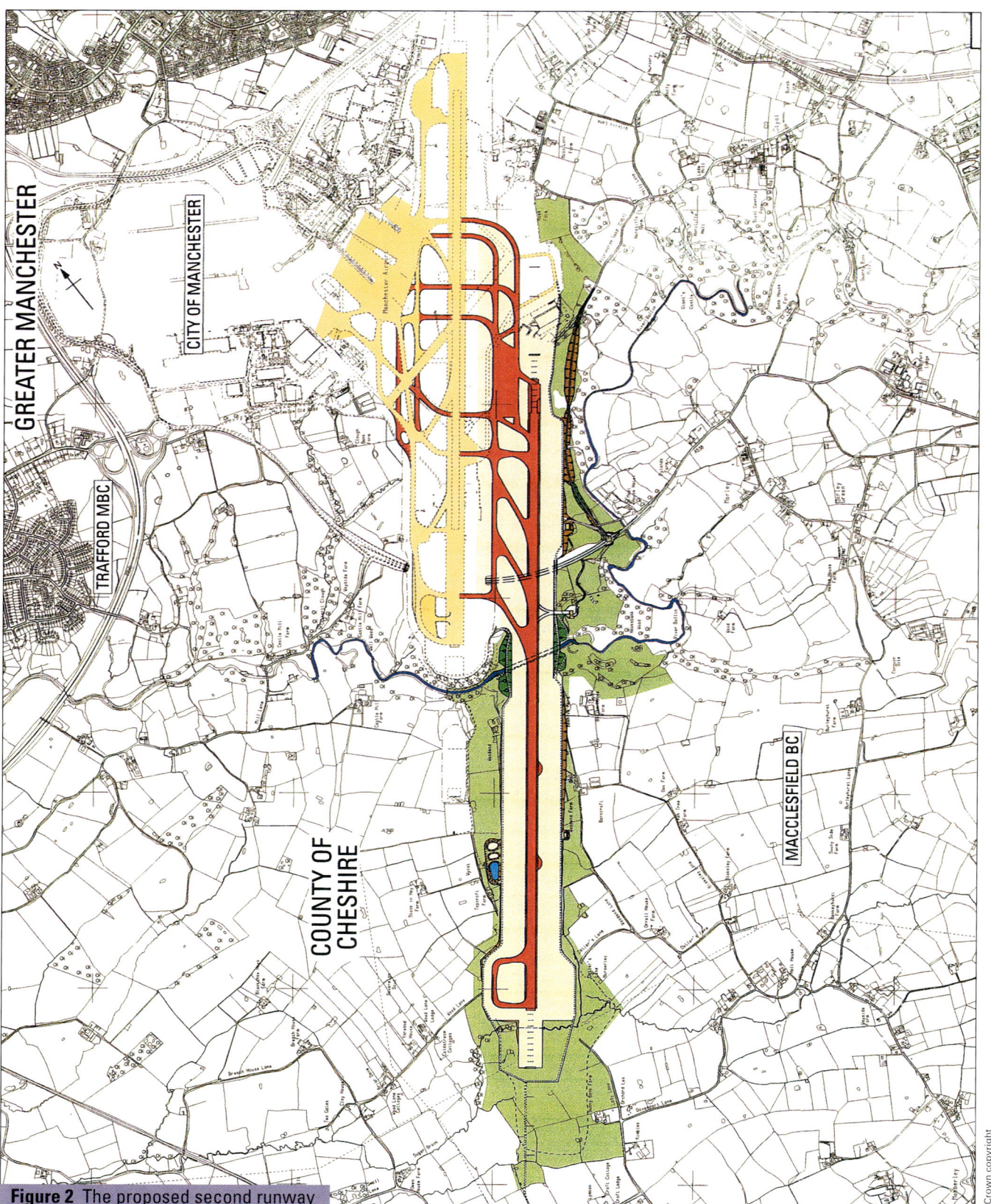

Figure 2 The proposed second runway

The runway itself

The second runway will be 3050 m long, parallel to and to the south of the existing runway (Fig. 2). The two runway ends will be staggered with an 'overlap' of 1850 m. The new runway will be mainly for departures.

The surroundings

There will be 324 hectares (ha) for landscaping, recreation and ecological works. There will be 35 ha of new woodland to replace the 6 ha of existing woodland which will have to be cleared. There will be 90 new or restored ponds which will provide wildlife habitats. The River Bodlin will pass under the new runway by means of a tunnel, and a weir will be removed from the river to encourage fish migration. Two listed buildings on the airport site will be demolished and re-erected elsewhere.

Figure 3 Aerial view showing the position of the proposed second runway

A second runway for Manchester Airport?

Public transport links

By 2005 the aim is for at least 25 per cent of passengers to use public transport to travel to the airport. To achieve this an interchange for bus, coach, metrolink and trains is being developed. Also, during construction of the runway, a rail extension will enable three trains a day to deliver a total of 1 million tonnes of stone from the Peak District so saving 185 000 lorry journeys.

Decision Making Exercises

What do people think?

> I like to use Manchester Airport when I can but often it means a change of plane at Heathrow, so really I would just as soon drive to London and get my direct flight from there.

MANCHESTER BUSINESS EXECUTIVE

> I am just sick of airport noise! I cannot enjoy my garden in the summer; nothing but aircraft!

LOCAL RESIDENT

> There is all this talk about landscaping and extra trees but what about the noise pollution? Let Heathrow cope with it rather than us.

LOCAL ENVIRONMENTALIST

> I want to see the airport expand. We already have a high reputation amongst passengers. The new runway could make our operation even more efficient.

AIRPORT WORKER

> Still more of our open countryside will be lost under a mass of concrete. What with all this land needed for new housing around Manchester and now this, there soon will be no countryside left! Let Heathrow take the flights! Surely a few hours' drive to get there is worth it if it means being able to save the countryside around Manchester.

LOCAL FARMER

> Manchester is the major city of northern England and needs an expanded airport if it is to attract more new firms. It would give a major boost to the local economy and make everyone more prosperous.

LOCAL POLITICIAN

A second runway for Manchester Airport?

FOUNDATION

1. a) Draw a line graph to show the likely increase in passengers using Manchester Airport.
   b) How many passengers from the North West have to travel to Heathrow or Gatwick in order to start their journeys?
   c) Why do they not use Manchester when it is nearer for them?
2. a) Suggest two reasons why Manchester needs a second runway.
   b) What economic benefits could a second runway bring?
3. Study the map of the airport (Fig. 2).
   a) In which compass direction does the existing runway run?
   b) Using evidence from the map, suggest why the proposed new runway is south of the existing one rather than to the north.
4. Using the information given, including the opinions expressed by local people, list the advantages and disadvantages of building the second runway.

HIGHER

1. a) Draw a line graph to show the likely increase in passengers using Manchester Airport.
   b) Suggest reasons why this growth is expected.
2. a) Suggest three reasons why Manchester needs a second runway.
   b) Explain how a second runway could be of benefit to the whole of northern England.
3. Study the map of the airport (Fig. 2).
   a) What evidence is there that great attention will be given to the environment if the second runway is built?
   b) Try to explain
   i) the alignment of the original runway
   ii) why the design for the second runway involves a considerable 'overlap' with the first runway.
4. Imagine that you have to speak either in favour or against the proposed new runway. Prepare your argument and decide how you would answer those who take the opposite viewpoint.

Decision Making Exercises

The options

 Option 1 – Build a second runway at Manchester so encouraging the economic expansion of the North West

Figure 4 Manchester Airport is used increasingly by foreign airlines

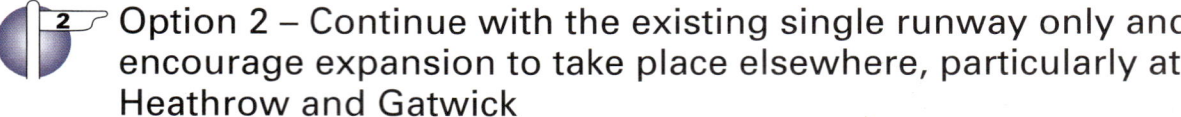 Option 2 – Continue with the existing single runway only and encourage expansion to take place elsewhere, particularly at Heathrow and Gatwick

Figure 5 Inside the terminal building

The Decision

FOUNDATION

You have to decide which of the two options you support.
1 Choose which option you prefer and give reasons in support of your choice.
2 Explain why you rejected the alternative option.

HIGHER

You have to decide which of the two options you support.
1 Chose which option you prefer and give reasons in support of your choice.
2 Explain why you rejected the alternative option.

Summary

Like Heathrow and Gatwick, Manchester Airport has experienced tremendous growth in the number of flights and passengers over the past 20 years. It has also become the major airport for northern England, offering an increasing number of international, as well as domestic, flights. By the late 1990s it has almost reached full capacity and, unless a second runway is built, it could mean stagnation instead of continued growth.

Understandably, the proposal for the second runway has had a mixed reception because of the inevitable conflict between economic growth and protection of the environment. Is it possible to build the runway and satisfy the environmental lobby? The decision at Manchester is one that could be repeated for many of the world's airports.

3 How should Riverside be redeveloped?

Background information

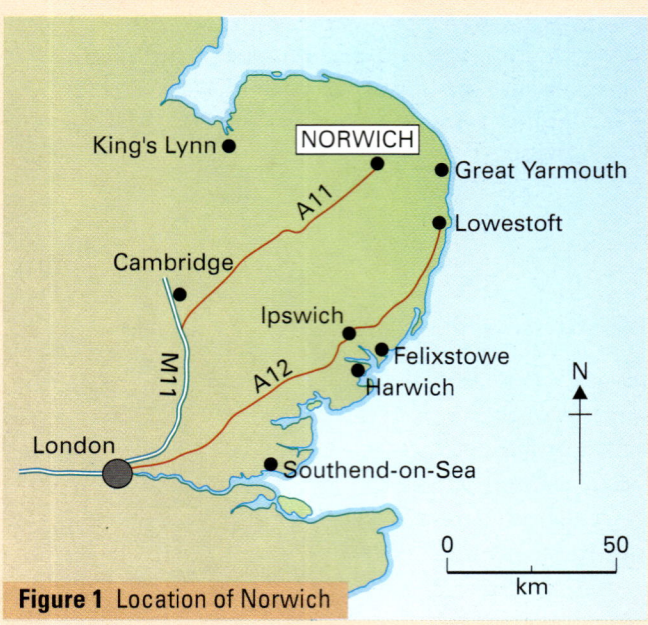

Figure 1 Location of Norwich

Riverside is an area of 19 hectares (ha) in the south-eastern part of the city of Norwich in Norfolk (Fig. 1), alongside the main railway station (Figs. 2, 3 and 4). The principal occupants of the site were a Boulton and Paul joinery and engineering works, and railway sidings. These have been virtually cleared from the site which is now used as a temporary Park and Ride facility for 550 cars and for coaches.

Riverside provides potential for a major redevelopment and expansion of the city centre, creating space for new commercial and leisure uses for which no suitable and available sites exist within the central area. This, together with the prominence of the site, the extensive river frontage, and the proximity of the railway station, ensures the redevelopment will have a significant effect on the character and appearance of the city and how it functions well into the twenty-first century.

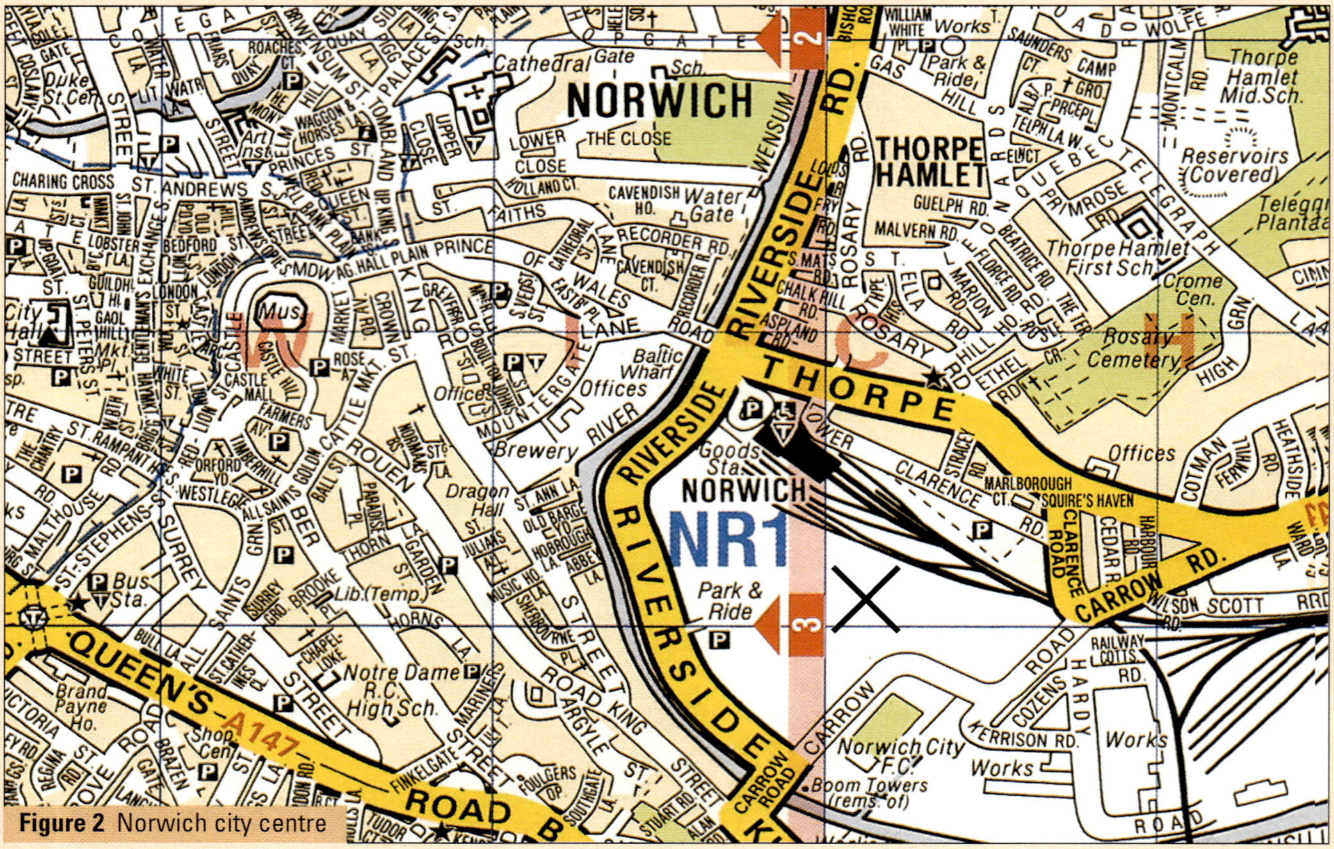

Figure 2 Norwich city centre

24

How should Riverside be redeveloped?

Figure 3 Aerial view of Riverside

Decision Making Exercises

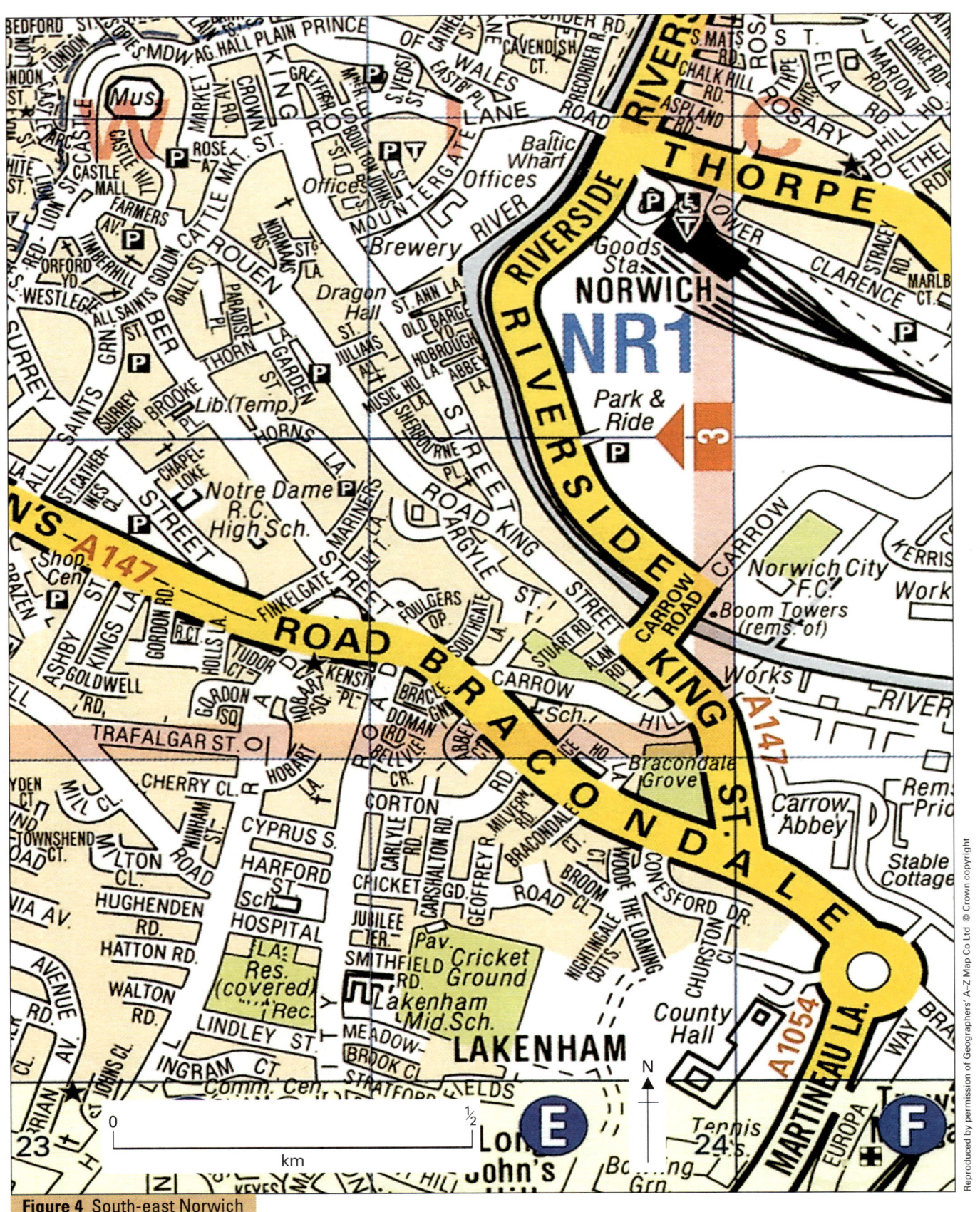

Figure 4 South-east Norwich

Planning guidelines

Retail

Norwich is a regional shopping centre, so any improvement to this facility will enhance the local economy. There is a demand for retail sites in the city centre. Food stores have tended to move out from the centre to the suburbs, and most parts of the urban area are generally well served. However, the south-east quadrant is not well served and there is a need for additional food outlets for people living in that area, as well as for the use of city-centre workers. Despite the downturn of retailing due to recession (at times 12 per cent of floorspace in the city centre was empty), there is still scope for the expansion in the number of small, specialist shops. However, such expansion must not be at the expense of the core shopping area, simply leading to a shift of location of the core.

Housing

Between 1988 and 2006, 7210 dwellings are planned for Norwich. Of these, sites for 4700 are already allocated leaving a need for sites for a further 2510 dwellings.

Tourism

Norwich is a focal point for the Broads National Park as well as being a regional centre for leisure and entertainment. In 1991 the estimated income from tourism in Norwich was £120 million with over 9000 employed (6000 full-time equivalent). The English Tourist Board identifies Norwich as a growing centre for tourism. Comparison with other historic cities suggests that the City of Norwich is under provided for in terms of hotels. There is room for at least one further 4-star or 5-crown hotel and a modern budget hotel.

Figure 5 River Wensum

Decision Making Exercises

Leisure

The City Council has identified that Norwich needs a leisure and/or competition swimming pool, an ice rink, a concert hall and a multipurpose leisure centre and sports hall. The heavy use of the River Wensum by pleasure craft (Broads cruisers, etc.) means that it is not suitable for water sports such as sail boarding and canoeing, but boat hire, excursions and water taxis together with mooring and landing facilities would all be appropriate (Fig. 5).

Employment

Office employment accounts for half the total employment in Norwich. However, due to the recession, there was in 1993 over 37 000 m^2 of vacant office space with planning permission for another 118 000 m^2. Therefore, it would not appear to be sensible to allocate a high percentage of the Riverside site to offices.

FOUNDATION

1. Look at the map of Norwich City Centre (Fig. 2).
   a) How far is the development site (marked X on the map) from the Cathedral?
   b) How far is the development site from the Castle Museum?
   c) What evidence is there on the map that the River Wensum has been an important transport link for industry?
   d) What other forms of transport are available for industry located in this part of Norwich?
2. Look at the map showing the development site (Fig. 6).
   a) What was the former use of the site?
   b) Name two features on the map which suggest that leisure facilities are available in this part of Norwich.
   c) What temporary use is being made of the site at the moment (Fig. 4)?
   d) List the main advantages which make this site attractive for redevelopment.

HIGHER

1. Study the map of Norwich city centre (Fig. 2).
   a) How far is the development site (marked X on the map) from the Cathedral?
   b) How far is the development site from City Hall?
   c) What advantages did the site have for manufacturing?
   d) Suggest one disadvantage the site has in terms of access to the city centre (other than distance) compared to other sites which may be closer.
2. Study the map of the development site (Fig. 6).
   a) What was the former use of the site?
   b) Using evidence from the map, suggest what leisure facilities are already available in this part of Norwich.
   c) Identify the present temporary use of the site and suggest reasons why it is being used for this purpose (Fig. 4).
   d) Why should this site be regarded as highly attractive for redevelopment?

How should Riverside be redeveloped?

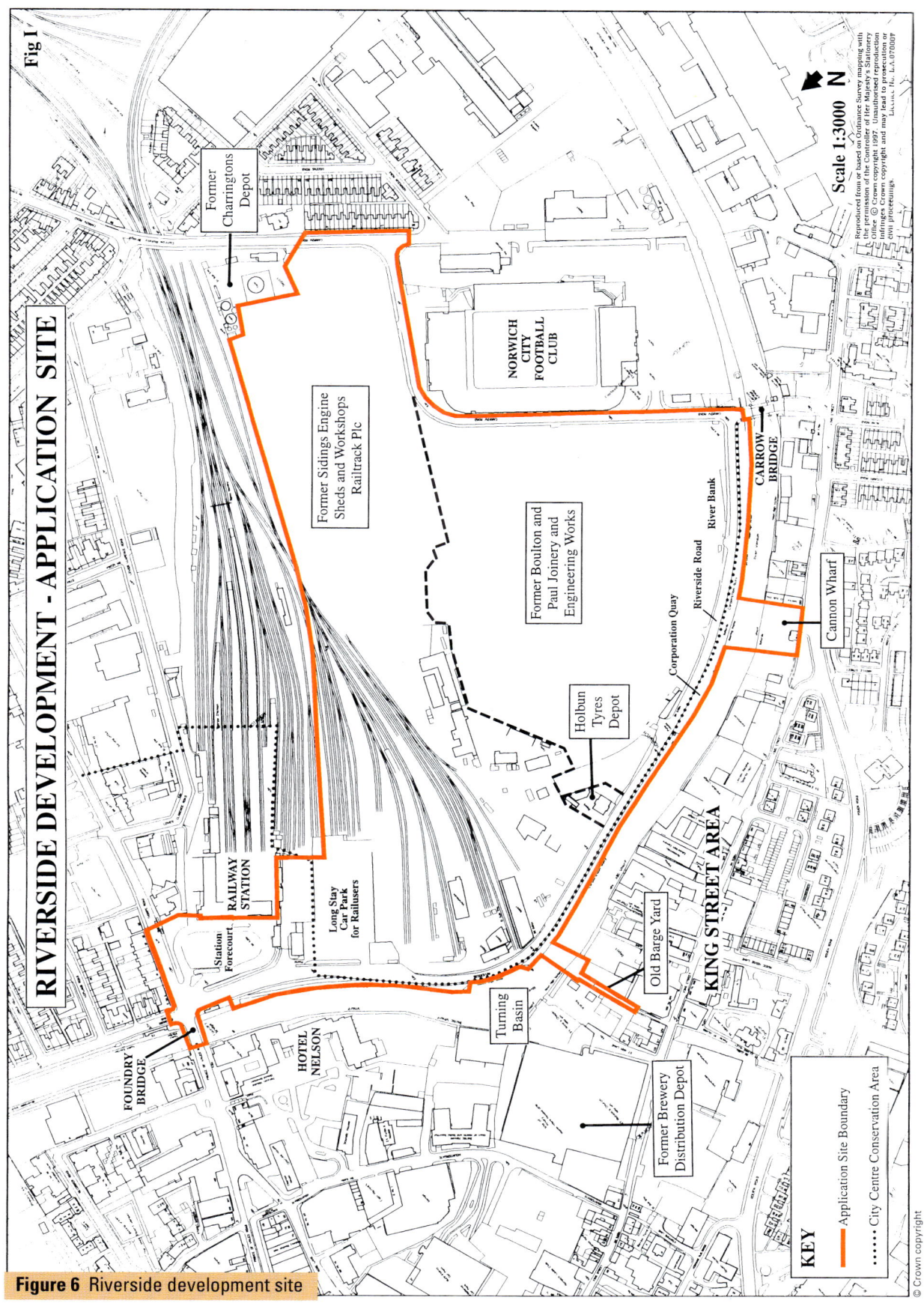

Figure 6 Riverside development site

Decision Making Exercises

Appropriate uses for the site – considerations

Figure 7 Proposed development site

- Excellent location in terms of access – alongside the railway station with good bus service (Fig. 6). Both pedestrian and cycle access could be improved easily. The site has an advantage over out-of-town locations particularly for those without private transport – potential car journeys are reduced so causing less environmental damage.

- Some retail outlets would provide the opportunity for comparison shopping with the main shopping core. A food store would satisfy the needs of the south-eastern part of the city and those living or working in the city centre.

- Leisure and entertainment facilities would benefit from the excellent access. Opportunities exist to capitalise on the river frontage in order to create a major attraction for both residents and tourists (Fig. 5).

- New hotels would benefit from proximity to the railway station, the city centre and views across the river to the historic core. In addition, hotel guests would be able to use any leisure facilities on the site.

- Housing provision would enable people to live near their place of work so reducing their reliance on the car with a consequent reduction in pollution, etc.

- A consideration for any office provision would be the proximity of the railway station, ideal for any workers who may wish to commute.

- The existing Riverside Road (Fig. 8) could be diverted around the eastern edge of the site so giving the whole site direct access to the river bank, with tremendous opportunity for landscape enhancement.

Differing viewpoints

We don't need any more shops in Norwich, there are already too many empty shops in the city centre. More shops on Riverside will simply mean that others will have to close down.

Riverside used to provide jobs, both in the engineering works and in the railway yards. What we need is to see industry back there, not just shops or houses.

The site would be ideal for mixed leisure activities such as swimming, an ice rink and a good concert hall. Alongside the river they could be made really attractive.

A super site for hotels. We need more in Norwich if we are to capture our share of the expanding tourist market. Nearly 10 000 people already work in tourist-related jobs in Norwich and that could expand.

This could be an attractive shopping area for many of the office workers in the city centre. Pubs and cafés overlooking the river would be a real attraction.

What we need close to the city centre are more houses to bring back residents into the heart of the city. At night large areas are virtually dead, the daytime crowds having gone back to the suburbs.

Right alongside the football ground, why not make the whole site a sports and leisure complex. We could do with a large swimming pool for a start.

Norwich has terrific opportunities for tourism. Much more use could be made of the river here with gardens and leisure facilities alongside.

This part of Norwich hasn't got the big food stores that are found in other parts of the city. One such store at Riverside would greatly benefit us.

It is so well placed for transport, right next to the railway station and with good bus connections to all parts of the city

FOUNDATION

3 Choose three different viewpoints expressed about the redevelopment of the site and, in each case, list other points they might add to support their general view.

HIGHER

3 From the various viewpoints expressed about the redevelopment of the site, choose two contrasting ones and list other points that they might use to support their view.

Decision Making Exercises

Assessing the options for redevelopment

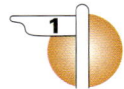 **Option 1 – Use the entire site for housing**

There would also be a small parade of convenience stores. This option could provide a good proportion of the land still needed for new houses in Norwich by 2006.

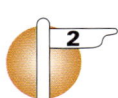 **Option 2 – Use the entire site for employment opportunities**

Employment would be mainly in manufacturing. As this site was formerly used for manufacturing, it would seem logical to continue with this land use.

 **Option 3 – Use the entire site for a range of leisure activities**

Norwich needs a whole range of new or expanded leisure facilities and this site would seem to be ideal.

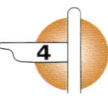 **Option 4 – Provide a mixture in terms of retail, leisure and housing facilities**

This would acknowledge that there are several equally important needs which could at least be partly satisfied by a mixed development.

Figure 8 Riverside Road

32

The Decision

FOUNDATION

Look at the list of options for the redevelopment of the site.
1. Choose the option that you think is the best and give your reasons why.
2. Choose the option you consider to be least suitable and give the reasons why you would reject it.

HIGHER

Study the list of options for the redevelopment of the site.
1. Choose the option that you think is best and give reasons for your choice.
2. Choose the option you consider to be least suitable and give your reasons for rejecting it.

Summary

The Riverside site in Norwich offers a rare opportunity to redevelop such a large area so close to the city centre. It has numerous advantages for a whole range of uses. Its position on the banks of a river means that it has landscape potential that is not often found in large urban areas, so perhaps leisure facilities should be given high priority in any redevelopment scheme. On the other hand, land is needed for housing and such a large site near to the centre of the city would seem to be an ideal way of curbing the unending drift to the suburbs. The site would also appear to have advantages for tourist developments such as hotels, and for it to become part of the retailing area of the city centre. All these varied possibilities need to be carefully considered so that the eventual redevelopment of the site can make the maximum contribution to the continued prosperity and quality of life within the city of Norwich.

4 Water management in Israel

Background information

Figure 1 Location of Israel

Israel is a small country. With an area of 20 700 km² (excluding the West Bank and the Golan Heights), Israel is only slightly larger than Wales. But there the similarity ends.

Climate

Since Israel was created in 1948 water, that is to say the lack of it, has always been a problem. As Figure 1 shows, Israel is situated in the Middle East, one of the largest arid regions of the world. Much of Israel (about 60 per cent) receives little rain and is desert (Fig. 2). The statistics in Figure 3 show another characteristic of the rainfall: its seasonal distribution. What neither the map nor the statistics show is that rainfall is very unreliable and that amounts vary from year to year. This variability, together with marked seasonal differences, makes water management a difficult task.

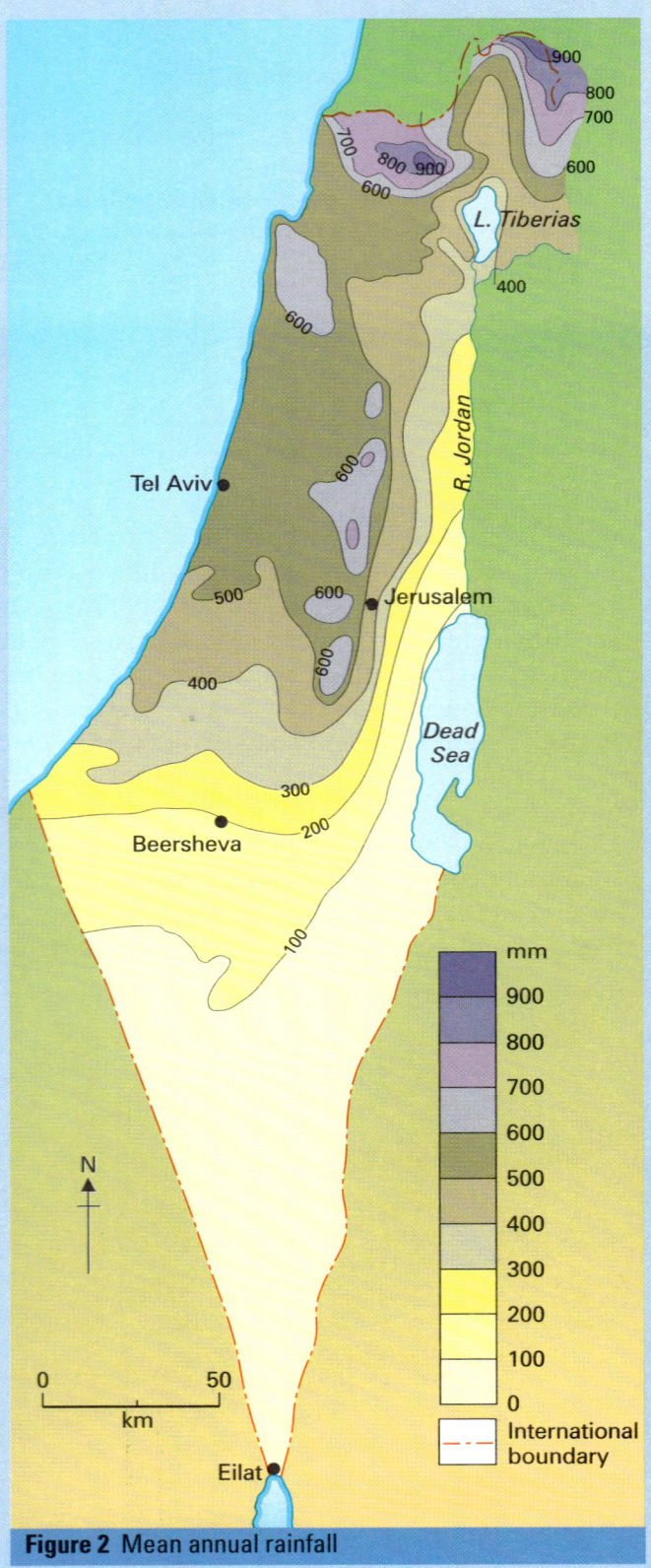

Figure 2 Mean annual rainfall

34

Water management in Israel

	J	F	M	A	M	J	J	A	S	O	N	D	Total
Tel Aviv													
Temperature °C: min	9	10	11	14	16	20	22	22	21	18	14	11	
max	17	18	20	23	24	27	29	30	29	27	23	19	
Precipitation: days	12	11	6	1	1	–	–	–	–	2	5	10	48
mm	130	88	51	18	3	–	–	–	1	31	81	136	539
Jerusalem													
Temperature °C: min	4	5	7	10	13	15	17	17	16	14	10	6	
max	12	13	16	21	25	28	29	29	28	25	19	14	
Precipitation: days	10	11	7	1	2	–	–	–	–	2	6	9	48
mm	148	120	97	29	3	1	–	–	–	21	70	116	605
Beersheva													
Temperature °C: min	6	7	9	12	14	17	19	19	17	15	11	7	
max	16	18	21	26	29	32	33	33	31	29	23	18	
Precipitation: days	8	7	4	–	1	–	–	–	–	–	2	5	27
mm	53	38	30	14	3	–	–	–	–	7	20	42	207
Eilat													
Temperature °C: min	9	11	14	18	21	24	24	25	24	20	16	11	
max	21	24	26	31	35	38	39	39	36	33	27	22	
Precipitation: days	3	–	1	–	–	–	–	–	–	1	–	1	6
mm	5	4	4	3	1	–	–	–	–	3	4	6	30

Figure 3 Climate statistics

FOUNDATION

1 List three problems linked with rainfall.
2 Look at Figure 2. Which areas receive
   a) most rainfall, b) least rainfall?
3 a) Look at Figure 3. During which months does Tel Aviv receive rain? In which months is there drought?
   b) Demands for water are greatest in July and August. Why is this a problem for water management?

HIGHER

1 Explain how the rainfall distribution creates problems for water management. Make use of Figures 2 and 3 to support your answer.
2 Study the temperature statistics (Fig. 3). What effect will the summer temperatures have on surface water supplies?

Decision Making Exercises

Water resources

Environmental Issues
SPRING 1997

WATER RESOURCES

Water is a scarce resource. Our freshwater supply is obtained from both surface water sources and from groundwater reserves. Both of these sources depend ultimately on rainfall, much of which is lost through evaporation.

Surface water

Israel has few perennial rivers. The main river is the Jordan, a small river by world standards. Its average annual flow is only 2 per cent that of the Nile.

Three main headstreams rising at 2000 m on Mount Hermon converge 25 km north of Lake Tiberias (Sea of Galilee) to form the Upper Jordan (Fig. 4). While the Upper Jordan carries much water in winter and spring, from April through to November it is little more than a brook. A short distance south of Lake Tiberias the Lower Jordan is joined by its tributary, the Yarmuk. The Lower Jordan is always a brook.

Israel's surface water is taken from the Upper Jordan by pumping it from Lake Tiberias (Fig. 5), the country's only natural reservoir. It has a storage capacity of 670 mcm, that is over a year's inflow, and it supplies half our drinking water. Much water is lost from Lake Tiberias through evaporation.

Problems for increasing future supplies include the high cost of constructing reservoirs. The fact that the tributaries of the Jordan rise outside Israel's borders poses yet another problem in terms of procuring adequate supplies of surface water (Fig.4).

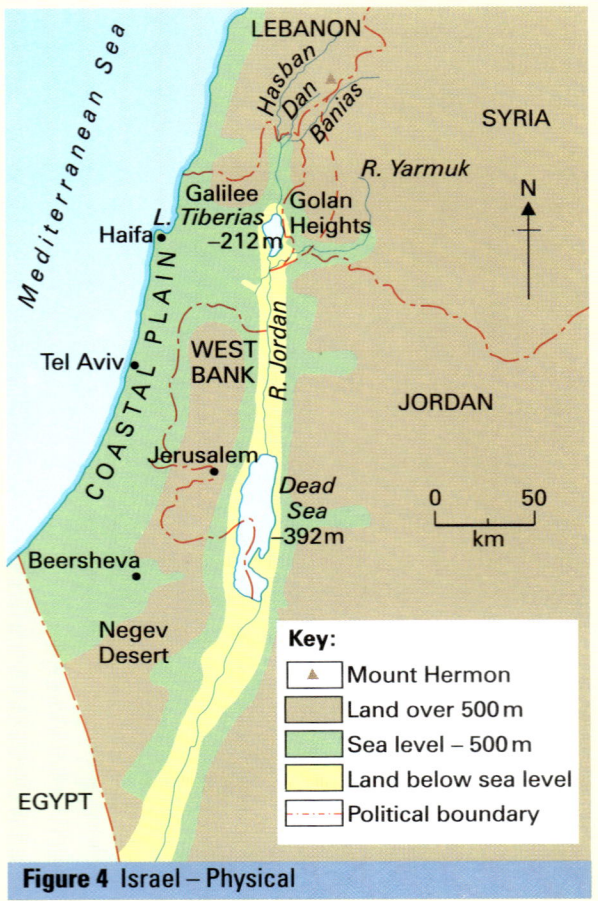

Figure 4 Israel – Physical

Figure 5 Lake Tiberias

Groundwater

Groundwater is the most important source of water for Israel, the West Bank and Gaza. Figure 6 shows the two main **aquifers**. The West Bank mountain aquifers are mainly porous limestone. Rain falling on these uplands (Fig. 6) emerges as springs in coastal Israel especially near Tel Aviv.

Figure 6 Water resources and transfer schemes

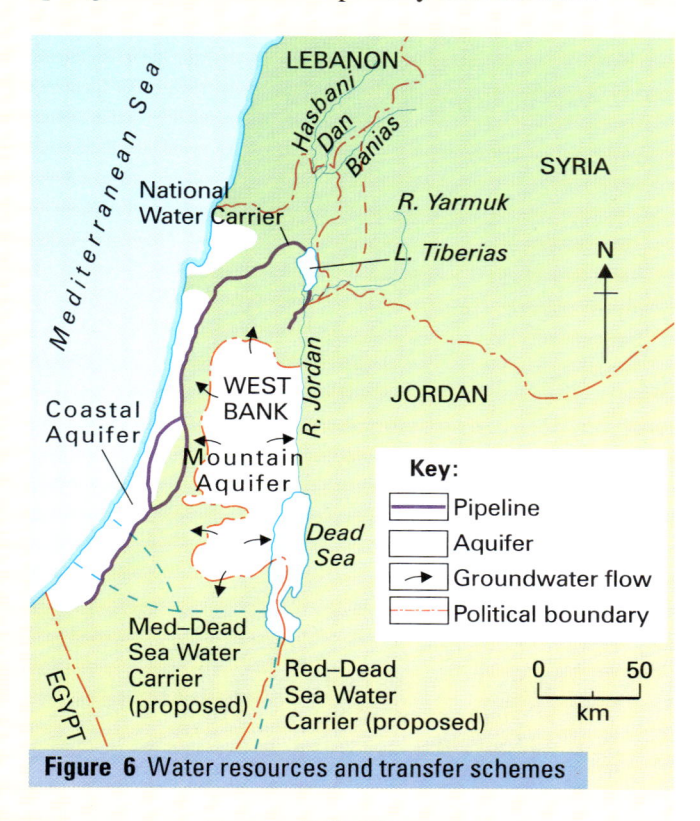

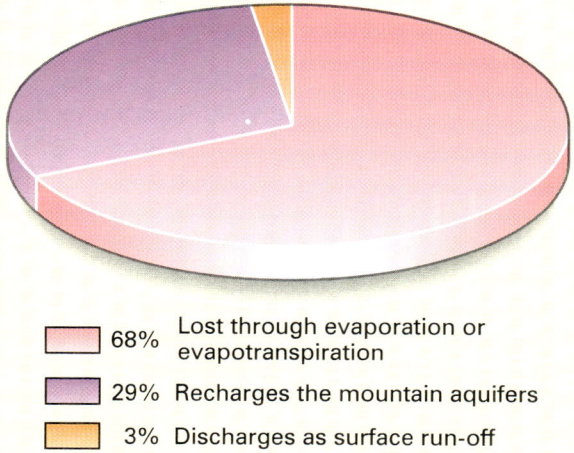

- 68% Lost through evaporation or evapotranspiration
- 29% Recharges the mountain aquifers
- 3% Discharges as surface run-off

Figure 7 Much of our rainfall is lost through evaporation, as the pie chart shows

National Water Carrier

Because of the lack of water in the Negev the Israeli government decided to build an ambitious water transfer scheme in the early 1960s. Figure 8 shows a section of the National Water Carrier.

National Water Carrier: fact file

- National Water Carrier takes water from the Jordan Valley to the coastal plain, a densely populated region where 50 per cent of the population lives, and then on to the Negev – a distance of approximately 250 km.
- A network of giant pipes, tunnels, open canals, aqueducts and pumping stations helps to transfer the water.
- It has never been an economically viable source of water for agriculture.
- It is high-cost water because of the high cost of pumping water out of the Jordan Valley.
- An estimated 16 per cent of Israeli energy costs was devoted to operating the Water Carrier in the late 1980s.

Figure 8 National Water Carrier

Decision Making Exercises

Figure 9 Development of water resources and water demand, 1947–93

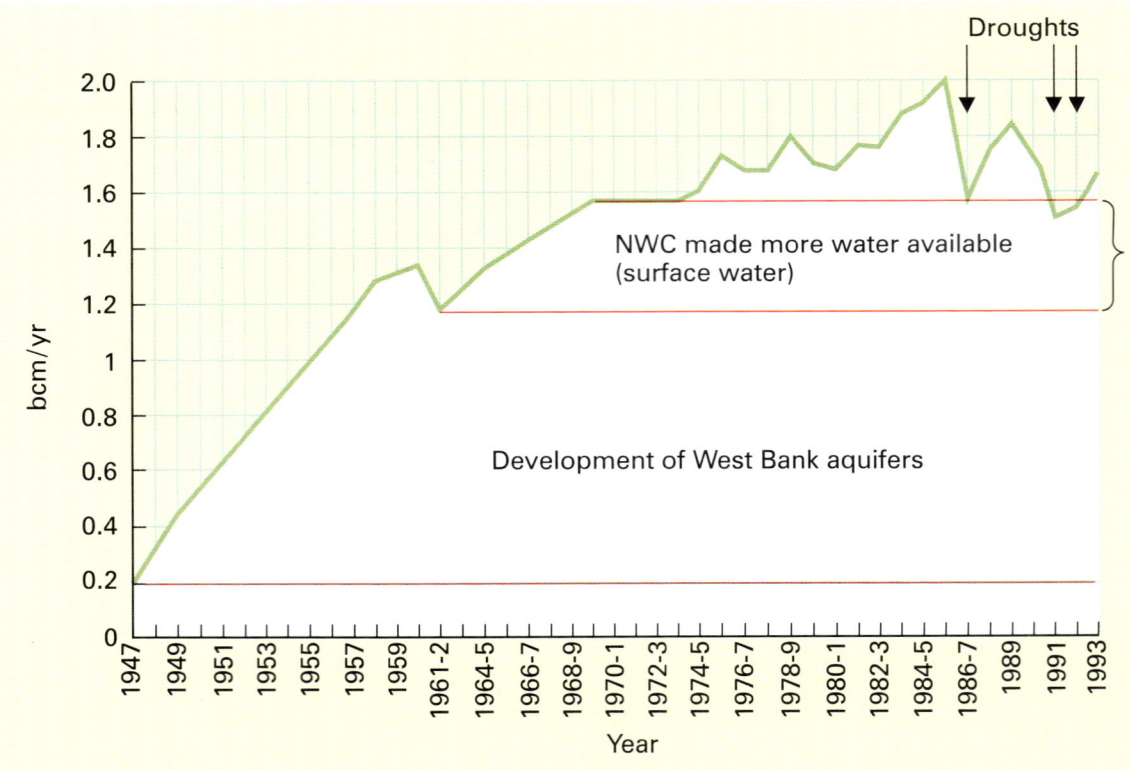

Note the rapid development of water resources in the first ten years of Israel's existence. The safe use of water is now 1.6 bcm/year.

FOUNDATION

1. a) Which is the main source of water for Israel?
   b) Explain what is meant by the term aquifer.
   c) Name a rock which acts as an aquifer.
2. a) Name the only natural reservoir in Israel.
   b) Which river flows into it?
3. Study Figure 8 and explain why pumping stations are necessary along the National Water Carrier.
4. a) Do you think an open canal is an efficient way of transporting water in a country with high summer temperatures?
   b) Give a reason for your answer.
5. Look at Figure 9.
   a) How much water can Israel safely use each year?
   b) How much water does the National Water Carrier make available?
   c) How much water is obtained from the West Bank aquifers?

HIGHER

1. Using Figure 6, where is the water source for the National Water Carrier?
2. Why is the cost of pumping so high?
3. Study Figure 9. How much more water became available with the construction of the National Water Carrier?
4. How much water is obtained from the West Bank aquifers?
5. It was estimated in the 1950s that Israel's water resources would yield 4 bcm a year. What does the graph (Fig. 9) suggest is the maximum yield?
6. Suggest why the development of water resources since 1957 has been slower than that of the first decade.
7. Explain why it is difficult for Israel to increase surface supplies of water.
8. What climatic factor can seriously affect water supplies?

Water demand

The New Settler
31 December 1952

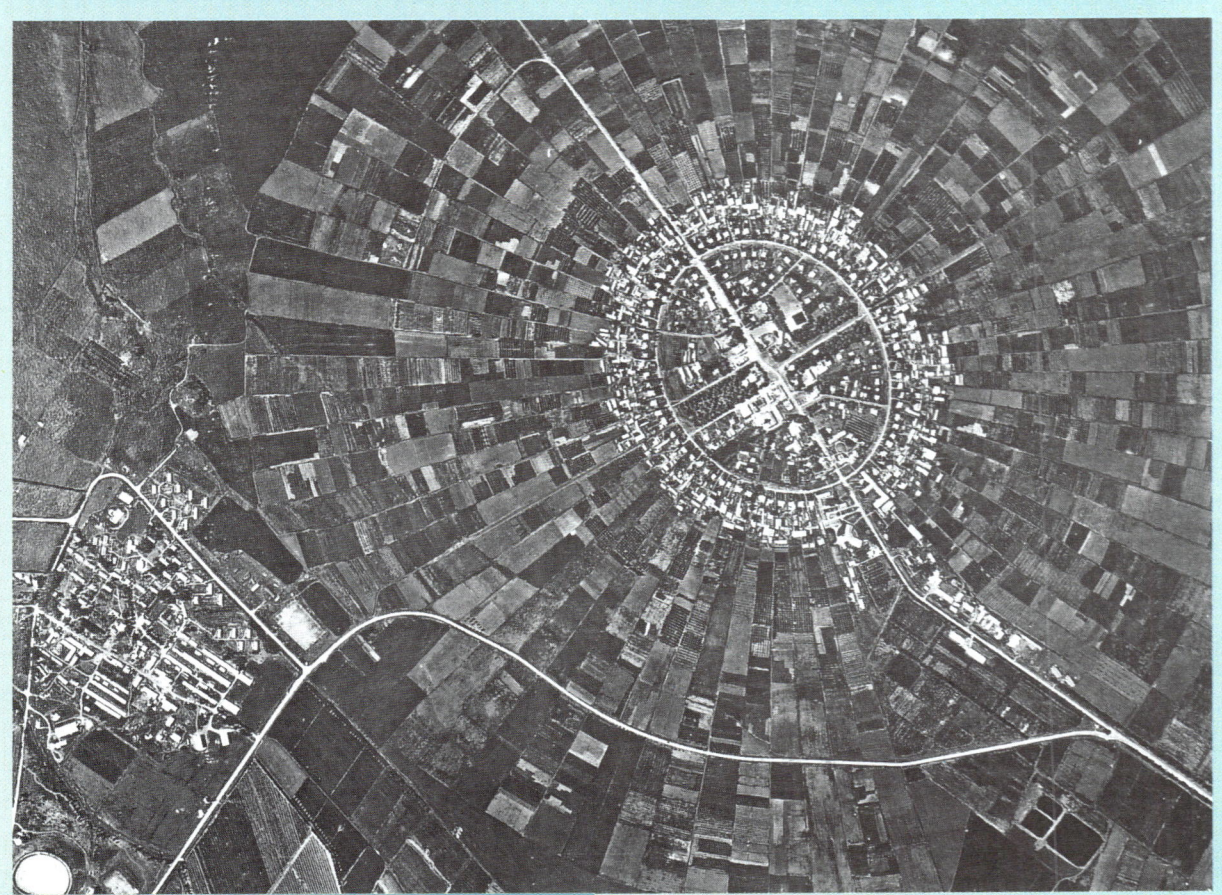

Nahalal Moshav: an agricultural settlement

The government announced that population figures had now reached 1.6 million. This rapid growth has been in part due to the influx of immigrants (nearly 700 000) and high birth rates.

Earlier this year our Prime Minister urged that we continue our policy of self-sufficiency in food. In order for our agriculture to be prosperous we must have large-scale irrigation projects. Without these we shall not be able to achieve high productivity, balancing the economy or economic independence. Water is the key to our economic development.

Water requirements

Drinking water: 1 m³/person/year (1 m³ = 1000 litres)

Domestic water: 100 m³/person/year

Food production: 1000 m³/person/year (if self-sufficient in a semi-arid climate)

New thinking

By the mid 1980s Israel's population had more than doubled that of the early 1950s (Fig. 10). Many people were becoming uneasy about the water situation. Pessimists estimated that the population could rise beyond 10 million by 2020. Some people felt it was time to introduce a new water policy, but not everybody's views were the same.

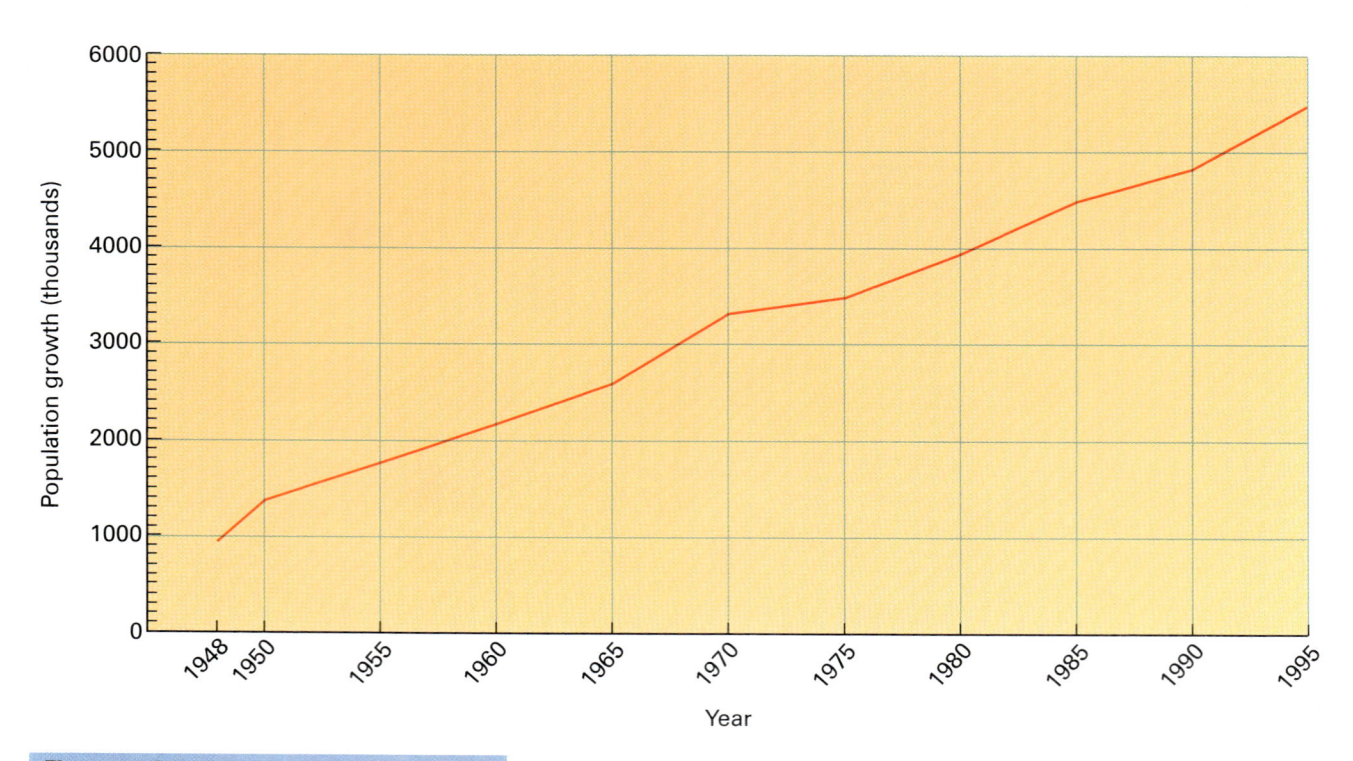

Figure 10 Population growth (thousands)

Exporting high-value water in water-intensive food crops is certainly not environmentally sustainable. Our West Bank aquifer is being overdrawn. We should be using our limited water resources more sensibly. (1982)

SCIENTIST

My livelihood depends on access to lots of water. We farmers irrigate field crops such as wheat and cotton – cotton is a really water-intensive crop – as well as citrus fruit, vegetables and flowers. Our national economic contribution is vital.

FARMER

We need to adopt a policy of allocative efficiency. This means that water goes to the sectors of the economy where economic returns will be greatest – industry, services, education. (1986)

GOVERNMENT OFFICIAL

Water management in Israel

Israel introduced other new ways of using water efficiently: water-saving equipment in homes and industry; improved irrigation techniques.
The re-use of waste water was to be increased.

A strong economy made it possible for Israel to take advantage of importing water-intensive food crops such as cheap grains from North America.

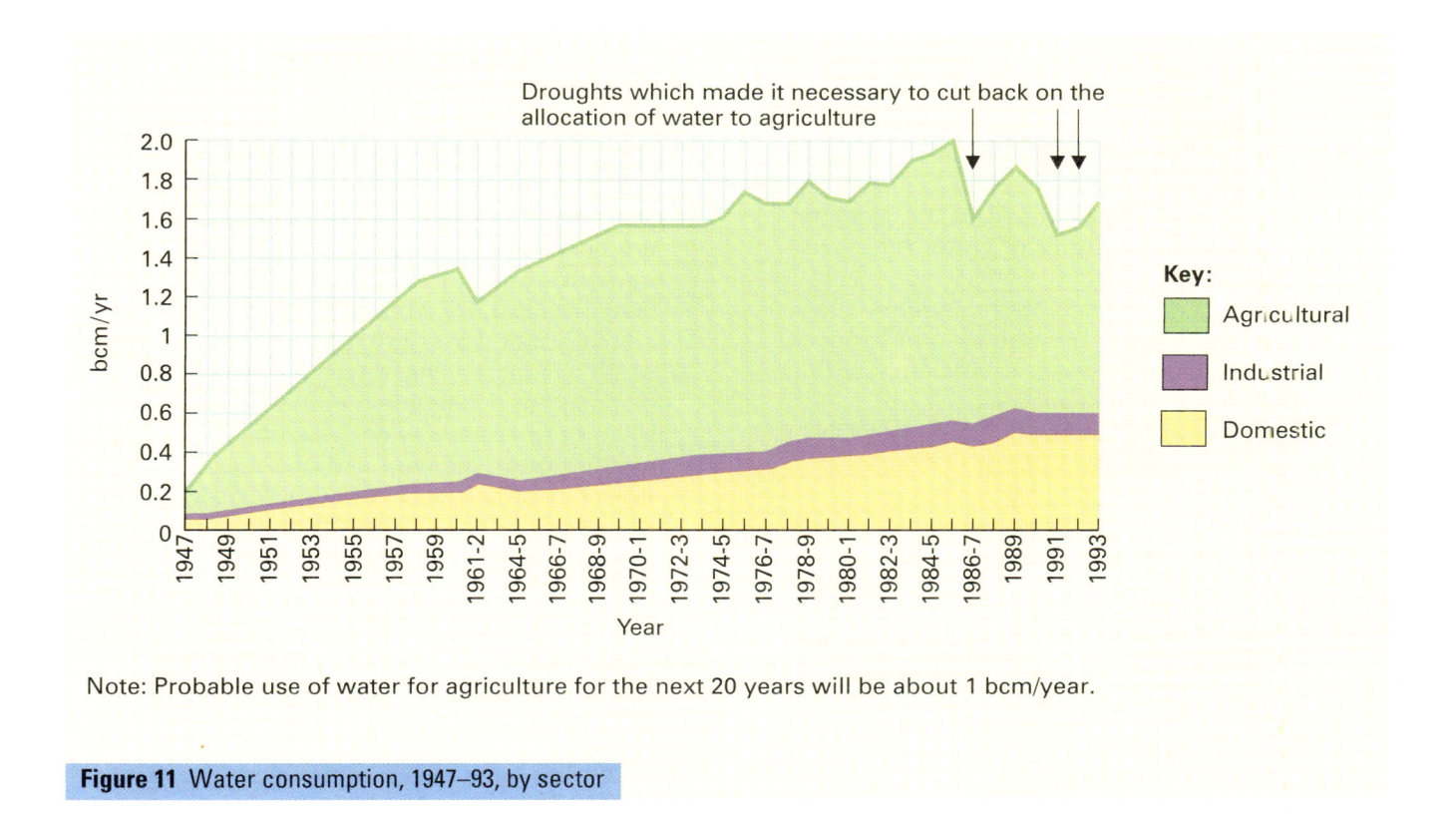

Note: Probable use of water for agriculture for the next 20 years will be about 1 bcm/year.

Figure 11 Water consumption, 1947–93, by sector

Figure 12 Tel Aviv: eventually the first use of water would be for domestic and industrial purposes. The majority of water in agriculture would be treated urban waste water.

41

Decision Making Exercises

FOUNDATION

1. a) What does the graph (Fig. 9) suggest about future water demand?
   b) Why is this going to be a problem?
2. Using Figure 11 state
   a) how much water was used by each sector in 1950
   b) how much water was used by each sector in 1993
   c) which sector uses most water.
3. Why was a change in the allocation of water necessary?
4. Why were farmers opposed to the plans to cut back on the amount of water for agriculture?
5. Why was it more sensible to increase the allocation of water to industry and services?
6. a) Why is increasing water efficiency within each sector a sensible idea?
   b) List the various ways in which Israel is making more efficient use of water.

HIGHER

1. a) What does the graph (Fig. 9) suggest about future water demand?
   b) Why is this going to be a problem?
2. Using Figure 11 state
   a) how much water was used by each sector in 1950
   b) how much water was used by each sector in 1993
   c) which sector uses most water.
3. Why was a change in the allocation of water necessary?
4. Why were farmers opposed to the plans to cut back on the amount of water for agriculture?
5. Why was it more sensible to increase the allocation of water to industry and services?
6. a) Why is increasing water efficiency within each sector a sensible idea?
   b) List the various ways in which Israel is making more efficient use of water.
7. How does the graph show that Israel has adopted a policy of allocative efficiency?
8. Suggest why Israel has taken a lead in the practice of water re-use and applying water tariffs.

The problem

The key issue is how to provide enough water at an acceptable cost and without harm to the environment in a country with increasing water demands but limited resources. All surface water which is politically accessible is being fully utilised. The only water available is groundwater, much of which is in the West Bank.

Water management in Israel

	1994	2000	2010	2040
Projected population growth (thousands)	5328	6544	7736	12 780
Water demand (mcm/year) — Domestic	545	687	890	1853
Industrial	129	130	155	255
Irrigation — Fresh water	967	896	642	579
Irrigation — Treated waste water	213	286	418	1054
Total water demand	1854	1999	2105	3741

Figure 13 Water demand planning

FOUNDATION

1 a) Approximately how many times bigger is the estimated population figure for 2040 than the population in 1994?
 b) Is domestic water demand expected to increase by the same factor?
2 a) Compare the amounts of fresh irrigation water with those of treated waste water for 1994. Which amount is the larger?
 b) Now compare the projected amounts of fresh irrigation water and treated waste water used in irrigation in the year 2040. What do you notice?

HIGHER

1 a) By approximately what factor will the population have increased in the period 1994–2040?
 b) By approximately what factor is domestic demand expected to increase in the same period? Suggest reasons for your answer.
2 Describe the changes in the relative importance of the use of fresh and treated waste water in irrigation over the period 1994–2040.

Decision Making Exercises

Assessment of the three options

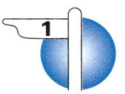

Figure 14 Improved techniques will reduce the amount of water used in irrigation

Option 1 – Increased water efficiency

- Further increases in efficient use of water in homes, industry and agriculture. In homes more efficient water-using equipment and domestic water tariffs will help reduce demand.
- Further cutbacks in agriculture and the increase of water re-use will mean that eventually the principal use of water will be for domestic and industrial purposes.

Option 2 – New sources of water

This will provide for industrial and domestic requirements only. It will come from a number of different sources:

- Desalination at the coast. This process is becoming cheaper ($1–$3/m^3) but it requires substantial energy input.
- Desalination on the Dead Sea. Major local pipelines would take water from either the Red Sea or the Mediterranean Sea to the Dead Sea (Fig. 6). These projects would be combined hydropower/drinking water schemes. The power would be used in the desalination plants. The Red–Dead project would cost between US $3.4 billion and US $4.2 billion, depending on the route chosen. It would restore and stabilise the water level in the Dead Sea. The water level has dropped dangerously low.
- Water imports by major international pipelines such as the Peace Pipeline from water-rich Turkey.
- Water imports using large vinyl water bags (still under development) and water tankers to move water from the water-rich areas of the Mediterranean (cost approximately $ 1/m^3 for 1000 km). There could be political constraints.

Option 3 – Increased water efficiency and new sources

The Decision

FOUNDATION

1. Decide which option you think will provide most water without damaging the water resource or the environment if the source is natural.
2. Give two reasons why you have chosen this option.
3. For one of the other options give one reason why you think this was not the best choice.

HIGHER

1. Decide which option you consider to be best.
2. Give reasons for your choice and state why you have rejected the others.

Summary

Israel is faced with a high demand for water which is not matched by its water resources. This situation has been caused by large-scale immigration and large-scale irrigation on the one hand, and on the other hand by climatic conditions and unavoidable political conflict. Political conflict makes access to resources outside the national boundaries difficult. A solution is water demand management. Various options are available but it is essential that the development of a water resource should have little negative impact either on the resource itself or on the environment.

Glossary

aquifer layer of porous rock storing and yielding useful amounts of water

bcm billion cubic metres

evapotranspiration water lost to the atmosphere through evaporation from the ground and by transpiration from plants

groundwater water found beneath the earth's surface; it is rainwater which has filtered through the soil and collected in the pores and cracks of rocks underground

mcm million cubic metres

5 Bodiam Castle

Background information

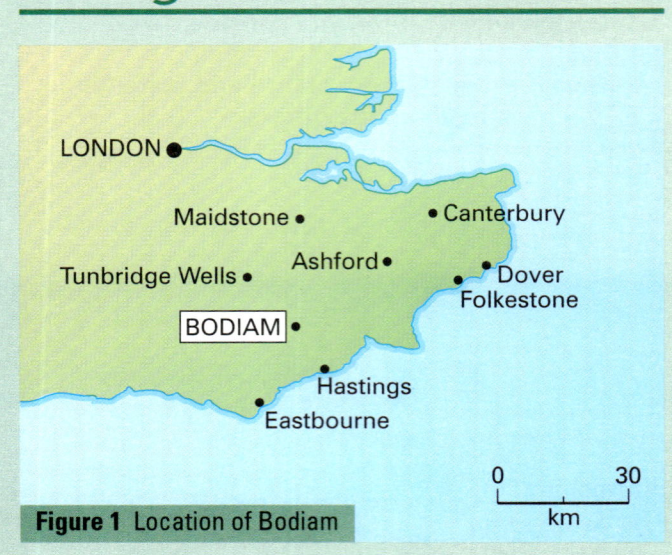

Figure 1 Location of Bodiam

Bodiam Castle is a major tourist destination in South East England, visited by nearly 200 000 visitors each year. Many of these visitors are from overseas, chiefly from France, Germany and the Netherlands. The castle was built on a site next to the River Rother more than 600 years ago when the threat of a French invasion was real. The castle was partly demolished during the Civil War in the mid 1600s, then fell into steady decay. Attempts were made during the nineteenth century to halt this process of decay, and in 1925 the castle was given to the National Trust. Today Bodiam is in the top-ten list of the most visited National Trust properties in the United Kingdom. Bodiam also attracts a large number of educational visits. Around 25 000 children and students in organised groups visit the castle each year.

Figure 2 Aerial view of Bodiam Castle

Bodiam Castle

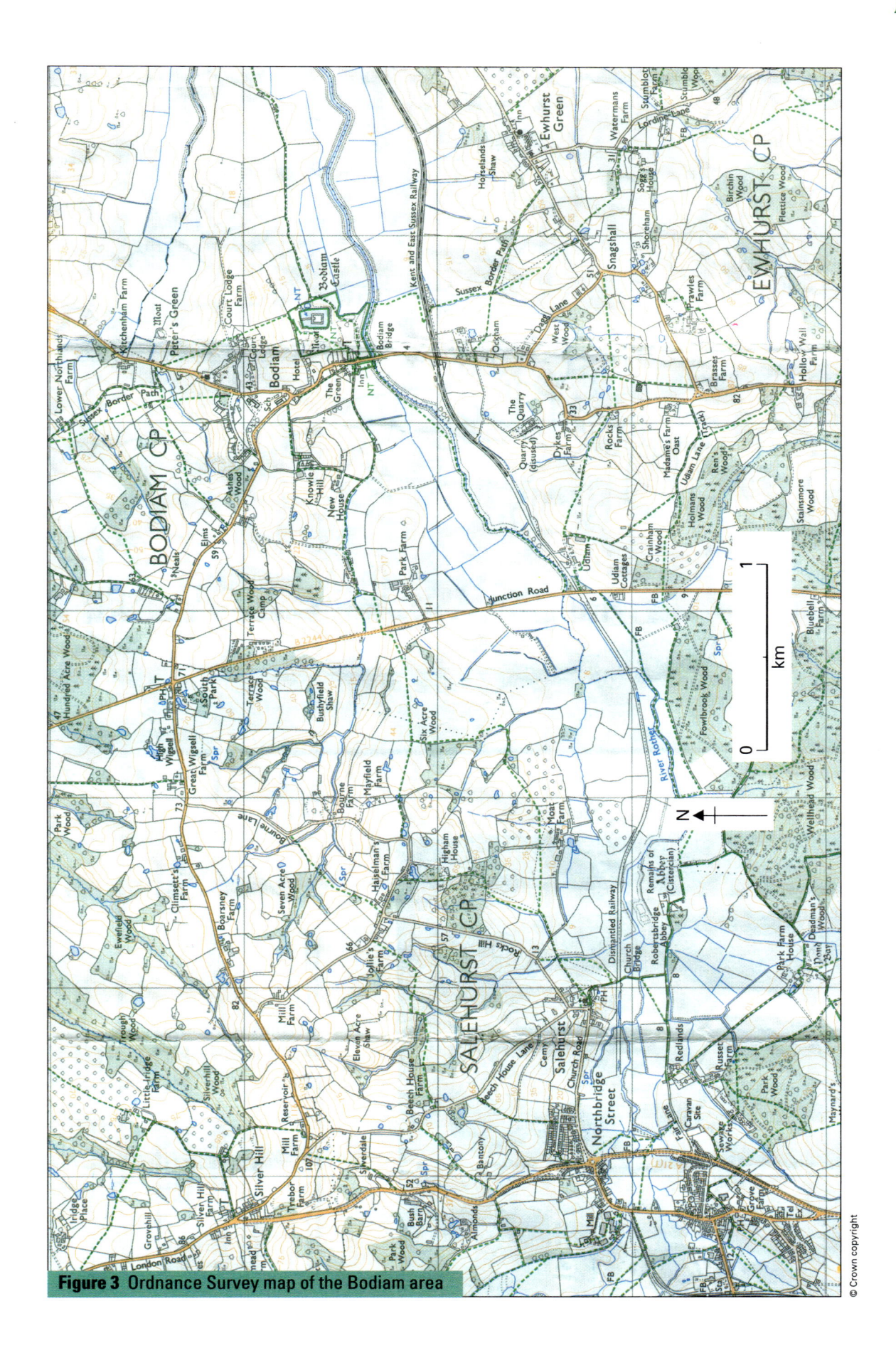

Figure 3 Ordnance Survey map of the Bodiam area

© Crown copyright

47

Decision Making Exercises

The issue

Visitor numbers are on the increase and the number of group visits is also increasing, both school parties and parties of adults, often from mainland Europe. Such parties arrive by coach: the only real access is by road (Fig. 3). Local roads, all of them minor roads, are experiencing a steady increase in traffic. Parking is available at the castle, although the amount of hard surface is restricted. This hard-surfaced area soon fills up if there are several coaches. Once it is full, cars can park on a grass surface, but this is not ideal if the weather is wet. On summer Sundays and Bank Holidays this grass area can become virtually full.

The village of Bodiam is small, the only properties directly benefiting from the visitors to the castle being a public house and a restaurant. Villagers and those living along the main approach roads are not keen to see a further increase in traffic, both cars and coaches, because the roads are so narrow (Fig. 3).

FOUNDATION

1. Look at the Ordnance Survey map (Fig. 3) which shows the area around Bodiam Castle.
   a) Which river is overlooked by Bodiam Castle?
   b) What evidence is there on the map that access to the castle will be difficult by coach?
   c) What evidence is there that reopening a railway line from Bodiam to Robertsbridge will be difficult?
   d) What evidence is there that the land alongside the river at Bodiam is likely to flood from time to time?
2. Look at the publicity leaflet for Bodiam Castle (Fig. 4).
   a) List the facilities that are provided for the visitor.
   b) At what time of year are the majority of special events held at the castle?
   c) Why is Bodiam Castle so popular with children?
3. Look at the aerial view of Bodiam Castle (Fig. 2) and find the overflow car parks as shown on the map (Fig. 4).
   What do you consider to be the main advantages and disadvantages of these overflow car parks?
4. Draw a simple sketch of Bodiam village and the castle, using the aerial view (Fig.2). Label your sketch to show some of the problems resulting from increased numbers of visitors to the castle.

HIGHER

1. Study the Ordnance Survey map which shows Bodiam Castle (Fig. 3).
   a) Which river is overlooked by Bodiam Castle?
   b) Using map evidence, suggest why access to Bodiam Castle is difficult.
   c) Using map evidence, list the main problems of reopening the former railway line between Bodiam and Robertsbridge.
2. Study the publicity leaflet for Bodiam Castle (Fig. 4).
   a) Why are most of the special events concentrated in one part of the year?
   b) What problems could be created by these events?
3. Study the aerial view of Bodiam Castle (Fig. 2) and find the overflow car parks as shown on the map (Fig. 4).
   a) As a visitor to the castle, list the advantages and disadvantages of using the parking areas during the year.
   b) Suggest why it would not necessarily be popular if these overflow car parks were surfaced with tarmac.
4. Using the aerial photograph (Fig. 2), draw an annotated sketch to highlight the main problems facing Bodiam Castle and Bodiam village as a result of the increasing number of visitors.

Present access to the castle

Road
- Private car – narrow minor roads linking with the A21 (5 km), the B2244 (2 km) and the A268 (3 km).
- Coach – again have to negotiate the narrow roads from the nearest A roads.
- Bus – an infrequent link to Hawkhurst and Hastings and sometimes to Eastbourne.

Rail
- The nearest mainline station is at Robertsbridge (7 km) with an hourly service to London but with no bus link to the castle.

Road/Rail/Road
- By road to Tenterden and then by the Kent and East Sussex Railway (Fig. 5) to Northiam (6 km), but there is no regular bus service to the castle. However, on certain days in summer, there is a bus (Fig. 6) or boat link (p. 53).

Therefore, apart from direct access by private car or private coach, other access to the castle is difficult.

EVENTS AT BODIAM

Special events for all the family – 10 reasons to come back for more! Regional Box Office telephone 01892 891001

28 March 1–5pm *Dragon Egg Hunt* The Easter Egg Hunt with a difference. No pre-booking – pay on the day £2.50

18 May *Spring Plant Fair* 1–4 Free exc. parking

25 & 26 May *All-Day Medieval Weekend and Archery Competition* Free exc. parking

20 June *Cajun, Blues & Boogie Woogie* Open air concert £10

21 June *Jazz at the Castle* with Kenny Ball and his Jazzmen £11 Combined ticket for both £20

19 July 6.30pm *Peter Pan* Illyria Theatre's production £8 adult, £4 child, £20 family (2 adults & 2 children)

20 July 11–4pm *Family Fun Day* Free, followed by 6.30pm Peter Pan Illyria Theatre's production, £8 adult, £4 child, £20 family (2 adults & 2 children)

28 July, 1 August am & pm *Jester and Circus Skills Workshops* Morning and afternoon sessions. For details and booking telephone 01580 830436 £5 per child per session

6 August *Stepping Through the Pages*. Meet children's authors etc. in conjunction with East Sussex Libraries. Free entry to event field. Free exc. parking

December *Christmas Cracker Hunt* telephone 01580 830436 after 1 Sept for details.

Birthday parties
Did you know you can book a children's birthday party at Bodiam Castle? Please call the Catering Manager to discuss details telephone 01580 830074.

Special offer
Travel back in time and come to Bodiam from Tenterden by Kent and East Sussex Steam Railway and 1950s RE bus. Tenterden to Bodiam return ticket and admission to Bodiam Castle – July, Sun and August Wed and Sun, adult £9, child £5. Telephone 01580 765155 for train times.

Figure 4 Publicity leaflet for Bodiam Castle

Decision Making Exercises

KENT & EAST SUSSEX RAILWAY – TIMETABLE 1997

MARCH
Saturday	1	8	15	22	29
Sunday	2	9	16	23	30
Monday	3	10	17	24	31
Tuesday	4	11	18	25	
Wednesday	5	12	19	26	
Thursday	6	13	20	27	
Friday	7	14	21	28	

APRIL
Saturday		5	12	19	26
Sunday		6	13	20	27
Monday		7	14	21	28
Tuesday	1	8	15	22	29
Wednesday	2	9	16	23	30
Thursday	3	10	17	24	
Friday	4	11	18	25	

MAY
Saturday		3	10	17	24	31
Sunday		4	11	18	25	
Monday		5	12	19	26	
Tuesday		6	13	20	27	
Wednesday		7	14	21	28	
Thursday	1	8	15	22	29	
Friday	2	9	16	23	30	

JUNE
Saturday		7	14	21	28
Sunday	1	8	15	22	29
Monday	2	9	16	23	30
Tuesday	3	10	17	24	
Wednesday	4	11	18	25	
Thursday	5	12	19	26	
Friday	6	13	20	27	

JULY
Saturday		5	12	19	26
Sunday		6	13	20	27
Monday		7	14	21	28
Tuesday	1	8	15	22	29
Wednesday	2	9	16	23	30
Thursday	3	10	17	24	31
Friday	4	11	18	25	

AUGUST
Saturday		2	9	16	23	30
Sunday		3	10	17	24	31
Monday		4	11	18	25	
Tuesday		5	12	19	26	
Wednesday		6	13	20	27	
Thursday		7	14	21	28	
Friday	1	8	15	22	29	

SEPTEMBER
Saturday		6	13	20	27
Sunday		7	14	21	28
Monday	1	8	15	22	29
Tuesday	2	9	16	23	30
Wednesday	3	10	17	24	
Thursday	4	11	18	25	
Friday	5	12	19	26	

OCTOBER
Saturday		4	11	18	25
Sunday		5	12	19	26
Monday		6	13	20	27
Tuesday		7	14	21	28
Wednesday	1	8	15	22	29
Thursday	2	9	16	23	30
Friday	3	10	17	24	31

NOVEMBER
Saturday	1	8	15	22	29
Sunday	2	9	16	23	30
Monday	3	10	17	24	
Tuesday	4	11	18	25	
Wednesday	5	12	19	26	
Thursday	6	13	20	27	
Friday	7	14	21	28	

DECEMBER
Saturday		6	13	20	27
Sunday		7	14	21	28
Monday	1	8	15	22	29
Tuesday	2	9	16	23	30
Wednesday	3	10	17	24	31
Thursday	4	11	18	25	
Friday	5	12	19	26	

Plus 1, 2, 3 & 4 JAN 1998

TO FIND THE TIME OF YOUR TRAIN

1. Please consult the calendar.
2. Each day on which trains run has a coloured background.
   NO COLOUR – NO TRAINS!
3. Read the timetable of the matching colour to see the train service running on the day of your visit.

ENQUIRIES AND FURTHER INFORMATION

Kent & East Sussex Railway
Tenterden Town Station, Tenterden, Kent TN30 6HE
Talking Timetable: 01580 762943
General Enquiries: 01580 765155
Special Events and Bookings: 01580 766428
Fax: 01580 765654

For details of train times from Northiam, please telephone 01797 253393
(please note this office is manned only on those days that trains run).

TABLE ONE – Standard Service
2 locomotives in steam

		*	V	*	V	*	V	*
Tenterden Town	depart	10.30	11.30	12.30	1.30	2.30	3.30	4.30
Northiam	arrive	11.03	12.03	1.03	2.03	3.03	4.03	5.03
Northiam	depart	11.20	12.20	1.20	2.20	3.20	4.20	5.20
Tenterden Town	arrive	11.55	12.55	1.55	2.55	3.55	4.55	5.55

All trains call at Rolvenden and Wittersham Road stations in each direction.
* = Steam train of 1930s and 1950s carriages including facilities for disabled passengers and trolley service of light refreshments.
V = Victorian steam train.

TABLE TWO – Off-peak Weekdays
1 locomotive in steam and heritage diesel observation train in action

		*	Diesel	*	Diesel	*	Diesel	*
Tenterden Town	depart	10.30	11.30	12.30	1.30	2.30	3.30	4.30
Northiam	arrive	11.03	12.03	1.03	2.03	3.03	4.03	5.03
Northiam	depart	11.20	12.20	1.20	2.20	3.20	4.20	5.20
Tenterden Town	arrive	11.55	12.55	1.55	2.55	3.55	4.55	5.55

All trains call at Rolvenden and Wittersham Road stations in each direction.
* = Steam train of 1930s and 1950s carriages including facilities for disabled passengers and trolley service of light refreshments.
Diesel = Operated by heritage diesel observation train.

TABLE THREE – Sundays
3 locomotives in steam May – September (2 steam plus diesel observation train at other times)

		Mixed	A	V	A	WB	V	A	V	WB	A
Tenterden Town	dep	10.30	11.05	12.15	12.50	1.15	2.00	2.30	3.20	3.45	4.30
Northiam	arr	11.00	11.40	12.45	1.20	2.00	2.30	3.00	3.50	4.25	5.00
Northiam	dep	11.20	11.50	1.00	1.45	2.10	2.40	3.25	4.05	4.40	5.20
Tenterden Town	arr	11.55	12.35	1.40	2.20	2.50	3.10	4.10	4.50	5.15	5.55

Most trains call at Rolvenden and Wittersham Road stations in each direction.
Mixed = Old-time mixed train – *passenger coaches and goods wagons!*
A = From May to September – steam train of 1930s and 1950s carriages including facilities for disabled passengers and trolley service of light refreshments.
 = March, April, October & November – heritage diesel observation train.
V = Victorian steam train.
WB = **Wealden Belle,** *luxury dining train.* Lunch served aboard 1.15 service, Kentish Cream Tea at 3.45. Advance booking essential for dining cars, limited accommodation for other passengers.

TABLE FOUR – Off-peak
1 locomotive in steam

		B	B	B	B	B
Tenterden Town	dep	10.30	12.30	2.30	4.10m	4.30k
Northiam	arr	11.03	1.03	3.03	4.43m	5.03k
Northiam	dep	11.20	1.20	3.20	5.00m	5.20k
Tenterden Town	arr	11.55	1.55	3.55	5.35m	5.55k

All trains call at Rolvenden and Wittersham Road stations in each direction.
B = Victorian steam train except in September when service is operated by a steam train of 1930s and 1950s carriages including facilities for disabled passengers and trolley service of light refreshments.
k = runs only in July.
m = runs only in September, October and November.

SANTA SPECIALS
Father Christmas and his band of pixies travel on these popular seasonal trains, distributing presents to every child and seasonal fare to adults. *ADVANCE BOOKING ESSENTIAL – BOOKINGS OPEN AUGUST*

Figure 5 Kent and East Sussex Railway timetable

How can the situation be improved?

Assuming most people want to use their own car, the car parking at the castle could be improved. If the grass area used for parking (Fig. 7) were to be covered by a hard surface, it could then be properly marked out as a car park. This would mean that 30 per cent more cars could be parked in the same area. However, it would mean the loss of the pleasant grass area for picnics. Although other grass areas are available, most visitors prefer to picnic on the grass alongside their car. Also because the hard surface areas at present are restricted in size they do not intrude on the attractive rural scene, whereas a large tarmac car park would spoil the environment. At the same time, some of the narrow approach roads could be widened so that the coaches, particularly the increasing number from mainland Europe, would have easier access.

Figure 6 KESR publicity leaflet

Make Tracks to Bodiam Castle
Available on Sundays in July plus Sundays and Wednesdays in August. Book in advance or pay on the day. Take a steam train from Tenterden to Northiam and then catch a 1066 Link Bus to Bodiam to explore this most fairytale of castles. Fully inclusive tickets: Adult £9, Child £5.

A Vintage Day Out
Combine first class rail travel with a chauffeur driven tour in a genui...

Figure 7 The existing car park at Bodiam Castle

Figure 8 A two-car diesel unit at Northiam Station

Decision Making Exercises

Figure 9 The narrow bridge across the River Rother at Bodiam

The rail line from Tenterden could be extended to Bodiam. At present it terminates at Northiam (6 km). A 45-minute service could be provided with each train carrying up to 200 passengers. There is space at Northiam Station (Fig. 8) for a 'Park and Ride' facility as there is room for 100 cars in the station car park (Fig.10). The track bed and track still exist even though the line has not been used since 1961. However, the track would need to be relaid. At present 80 000 people each year travel by train from Tenterden to Northiam. Why not encourage them to extend their trip to include a visit to Bodiam Castle?

Figure 10 The existing car parking area at Northiam Station

Another possibility would be to re-establish a rail link from Bodiam to Robertsbridge mainline station, so giving a direct rail link to London. After its closure in 1961 this line was removed and much of its track bed returned to farmland. Although the distance from Bodiam to Robertsbridge is virtually the same as from Bodiam to Northiam, not all the farmers may want to sell their land back to the railway. Also, since 1961, a bypass around Robertsbridge has been built which cuts right through the line of the former track, so an expensive bridge would be needed. A level crossing would be cheaper but would cause major hold-ups on the busy A21, London to Hastings road.

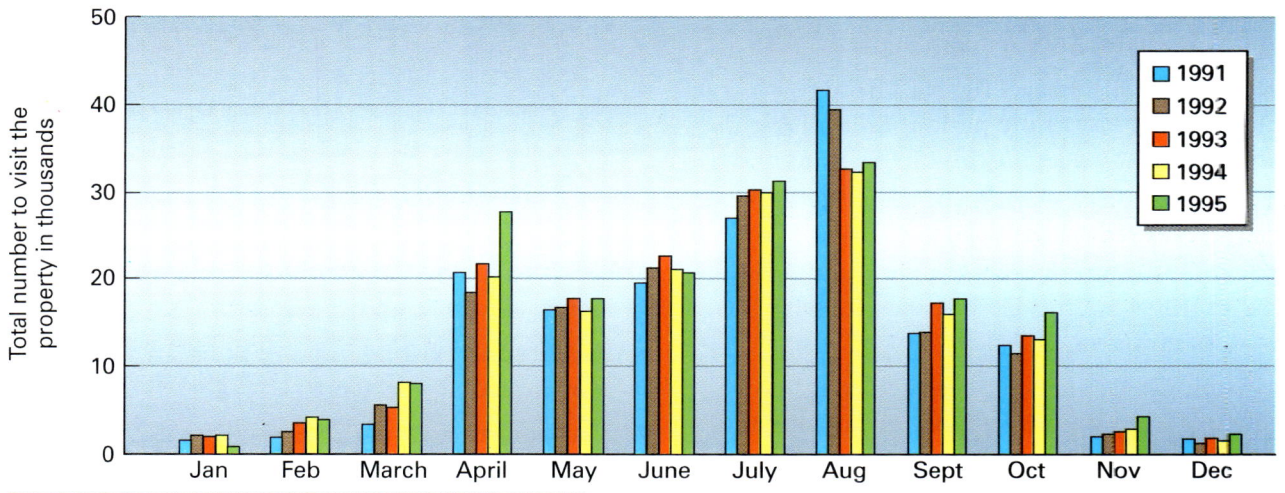

Figure 11 Bodiam Castle visitors by month, 1991–5

FOUNDATION

5 Look at the graph of visitor numbers (Fig. 11).
   a) On average, which seem to be the most popular months?
   b) Suggest why.
6 What are the main advantages of extending the Kent and East Sussex Railway line from Northiam to Bodiam?
7 Suggest why some people are against the idea of replacing the railway line between Bodiam and Robertsbridge.

HIGHER

5 Study the graph which shows the number of visitors to the castle (Fig. 11).
   a) Why do the numbers in each month vary from year to year?
   b) Do you think the distribution of visitors throughout the year is ideal?
   c) Explain your answer to 5b).
6 a) List the main advantages of restoring the railway line between Bodiam and Northiam.
   b) What evidence is there that the Kent and East Sussex Railway is already trying to establish a link between Tenterden and Bodiam?
   c) Suggest why some people are against the idea of the restoration of a rail link.

53

Decision Making Exercises

Assessing the three options

Option 1 – Extend the Kent and East Sussex Railway from Northiam to Bodiam

- The track bed is still intact although not used since 1961 – this would need to be relaid with work on clearance, fencing and drainage.
- Bodiam Station still exists as it was in 1961. The idea is to preserve it as it was with no car parking provided, no gift shop, etc. People arriving by train would walk the short distance to the castle where gift shops and other facilities are available.
- Northiam Station has parking space for 100 cars. Road access to Northiam is much better than to Bodiam, as Northiam is on the A28.
- People could also travel by train from Tenterden where ample parking is available. Tenterden also has a bus link to Ashford and Headcorn, both of which provide a mainline link to London.
- Expertise, locomotives and rolling stock already exist as the Kent and East Sussex Railway has been operating since 1974.
- A 45-minute frequency of service could be provided; each train is capable of carrying the equivalent of four motor coaches.

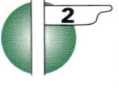

Option 2 – Rebuild the rail link from Bodiam to Robertsbridge

- This would provide a direct link into the mainline network from Hastings to London.
- Although the track bed has gone the land has not been built on and could be bought back from farmers.
- Although the Robertsbridge bypass on the A21 has been built since the line closed in 1961, a bridge or level crossing could be built.
- Locomotives and rolling stock could be purchased and expertise developed in order to operate the line.

Option 3 – Improve road links to the castle and create more parking space

- Widen existing narrow roads and straighten bends to make them more suitable for increased coach and car traffic.
- Replace the existing grass parking area with a proper tarmac surface.
- Mark out the car park area so that it will take more cars.
- Try to landscape the new car park to lessen environmental damage.

Figure 12 Bodiam Castle from Bodiam station

54

The Decision

FOUNDATION

Look at the three options for improving access to Bodiam Castle.
1. Choose the option you support and give your reasons.
2. Choose one of the options you rejected and explain why you rejected it.

HIGHER

Study the three options for improving access to Bodiam Castle.
1. Choose the option that you consider to be the best and explain your reasons.
2. Explain why you rejected the other two options.

Summary

Bodiam Castle in East Sussex is a major tourist attraction being in the top-ten most visited National Trust properties. The castle's position is relatively remote in terms of modern road and rail communications; it is accessible by road only by means of narrow country lanes. Since the opening of the Channel Tunnel there has been a marked increase in the number of foreign visitors, especially coach parties. This increase in coach traffic as well as the increase in private car traffic is likely to present growing problems for those responsible for the management of the castle, as well as for those who live in the immediate area. Access to the castle needs to be made easier but how?

Should road access and parking be improved or should improvements be made to public transport so enabling visitor numbers to increase without the increase in road traffic which so often accompanies it?

6 Replacing sea defences in Herne Bay

Background information

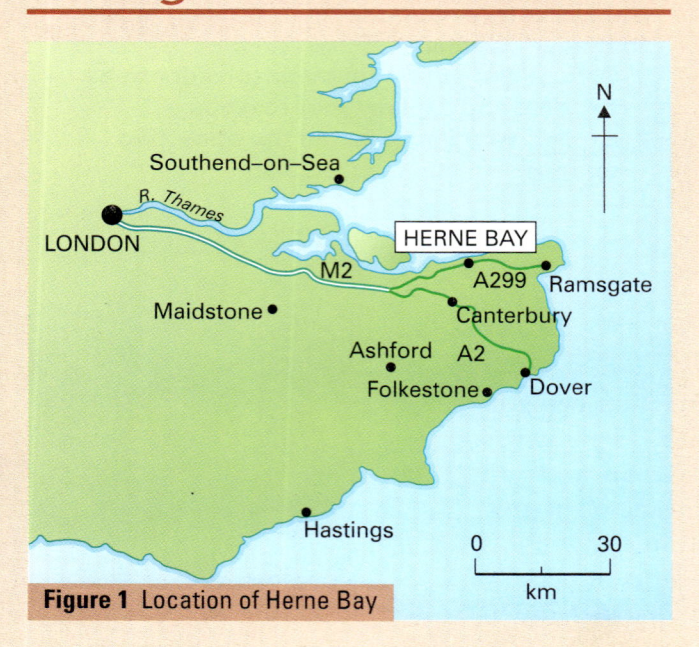

Figure 1 Location of Herne Bay

Herne Bay is situated on the North Kent coast. The coastline is aligned approximately east–west and is subject to wave attack from the North Sea, particularly when the wind is from the north. When strong northerly winds combine with a **North Sea surge**, sea level can rise by up to 2 m above predicted levels, producing exceptionally high tides. Consequently, serious flooding and damage can result. There has been a long history of flooding and coastal damage. More recently:

- In 1953 the worst flooding in living memory occurred (Fig. 2).
- In December 1976 a force 10 gale caused paving stones to be thrown up and smashed, shelters were damaged, railings were buckled and broken, part of the edge of the promenade fell into the sea, groynes were badly damaged and tonnes of shingle were thrown on to the road and pavement.
- In the great storm of December 1978 the sea front was severely damaged and most of the 1.2 km-long pier was destroyed.

Figure 2 Flood damage on Herne Bay sea front, 1953

Replacing sea defences in Herne Bay

Figure 3 Storm conditions on Herne Bay sea front

Canterbury City Council, responsible for this section of coastline, has a coastal management policy whereby defences are renewed over a 50-year period. It was decided that the defences from the pier to William Street should be given high priority. They were in poor condition and should they fail land behind them would be flooded. Much of the town is built on low-lying land and flooding affects both residential and commercial properties (Fig. 4).

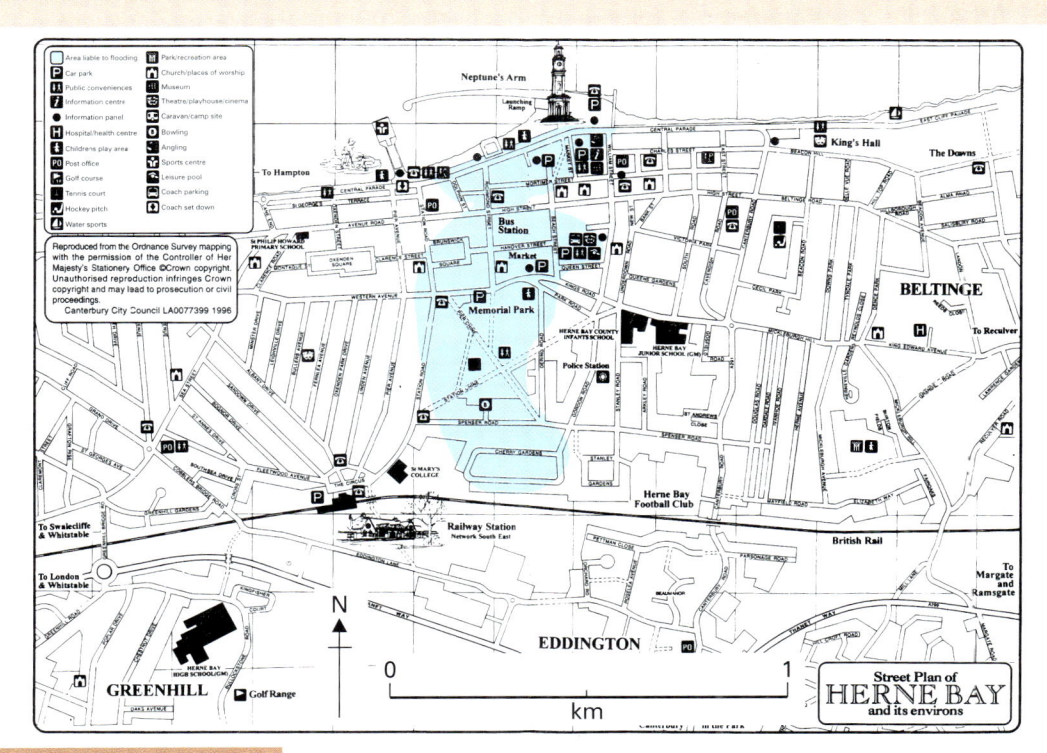

Figure 4 Possible extent of flooding

57

Decision Making Exercises

Several schemes have been proposed to try to protect the sea wall from damage and to prevent flooding of the land behind. The most recent proposals include an ambitious scheme which combines sea defence with plans to upgrade the sea front in an attempt to boost Herne Bay's tourist trade (Fig. 5).

The problem

The sea defences comprised a low shingle beach backed by a sea wall. These defences were inadequate for a number of reasons.

- The shingle beach, despite a system of groynes together with frequent beach replenishment, was continually being eroded and was too low to provide a good line of defence against storm waves. Instead of the waves losing much of their energy as they broke on the beach, they broke with full force against the front wave wall (Fig. 3).

- The front wave wall, built in the 1920s, was nearing the end of its design life. The low-quality concrete blocks having been subjected to powerful wave attack over a long period were in poor condition. The apron in front of the wave wall had also been broken up by wave attack.

- The rear wave wall was built in the 1960s on shingle. In the event of the front wave wall being breached, the shingle would have been washed out and the wall, although in good condition for its age, would have collapsed.

- The rear wave wall was not high enough to afford protection against a storm of the magnitude of the February 1953 storm.

In addition, two further hazards had to be considered.

- South East England is sinking at a rate of between 150 mm and 300 mm a century.
- The possible effects of global warming which would increase both the frequency and severity of flooding.

FOUNDATION

1. Which winds are the greatest threat to Herne Bay?
2. What can increase the height of the tide above its expected level?
3. Why has the beach not provided much protection against strong waves?
4. What structures have been built to protect the town?
5. List three reasons why these structures are no longer adequate.

HIGHER

1. What weather conditions cause extra high tides and flooding in Herne Bay?
2. Why does the beach not provide a first line of defence against wave attack?
3. Explain why it is necessary to replace the sea defences.

Figure 5 Herne Bay sea front

Assessing the options for strengthening the sea defences

When Canterbury City Council decided that the existing sea defences had to be replaced, it stipulated that the new scheme must be environmentally acceptable and economically viable (not too expensive). The scheme also had to comply with the following criteria:
- Flooding due to overtopping must not exceed 1 litre of water for every 1 m length of wall per second.
- The structure must be able to stand up to a storm of the same strength as the 1953 storm.
- The ongoing maintenance costs must be low.
- The scheme must not adversely affect any neighbouring stretches of coast.
- The scheme must be safe for the public.
- The people of Herne Bay must like the scheme.

The key factor in the protection of the sea wall against erosion and the reduction of overtopping is the beach. A major problem is that **longshore drift** is westerly and that the supply of shingle from the east is small. It was decided to consult a Dutch firm of coastal defence engineers because the Dutch are experts in this branch of engineering.

The options

After the first round of investigations, five options were put forward for further investigation:
1. Upgrade the existing defences
2. Rip-rap revetment
3. Widened shingle beach with groynes
4. Widened sand beach with groynes
5. Offshore breakwater with groynes either end to fix the beach.

All schemes would protect Herne Bay from flooding for the next 50 years. All would alter the appearance of the sea front. All would require repairs to the existing sea wall.

The Council invited the public to express their views. An exhibition was staged showing the plans for the proposed sea defence and landscaping schemes. Look at the information given in Figures 6 to 11 and read the viewpoints expressed by residents about the options 2 to 5.

Scheme	Cost £ m	Rear wall height	Amount of water coming over each metre of wall per second
Improve existing	4.0	higher	1 litre
Rip-rap revetment	5.4	same	2 litres
Widened shingle beach	4.9	same	3 litres
Widened sand beach	8.1	lower	1 litre
Breakwater	4.4	lower	1 litre

Figure 6 Results based on model tests and computer analysis

Decision Making Exercises

a) Plan View

Granite boulders weighing between 1 and 3 tonnes

Toe of revetment

Bandstand

Clock Tower Jetty

Neptune Jetty

Herne Bay Pier

Wide berm (20 m) Would be unattractive Would ruin Herne Bay as a tourist centre

0 100 200 300 m

b) Cross-section

Rear wave wall

20 m berm

Sea wall

Rock

1:1.5

Height A.O.D. (m)

Distance from sea wall (m)

NB Vertical scale 1:100
Horizontal scale 1:1000
Slope of beach exaggerated

© Crown copyright

Figure 7 Rip-rap revetment

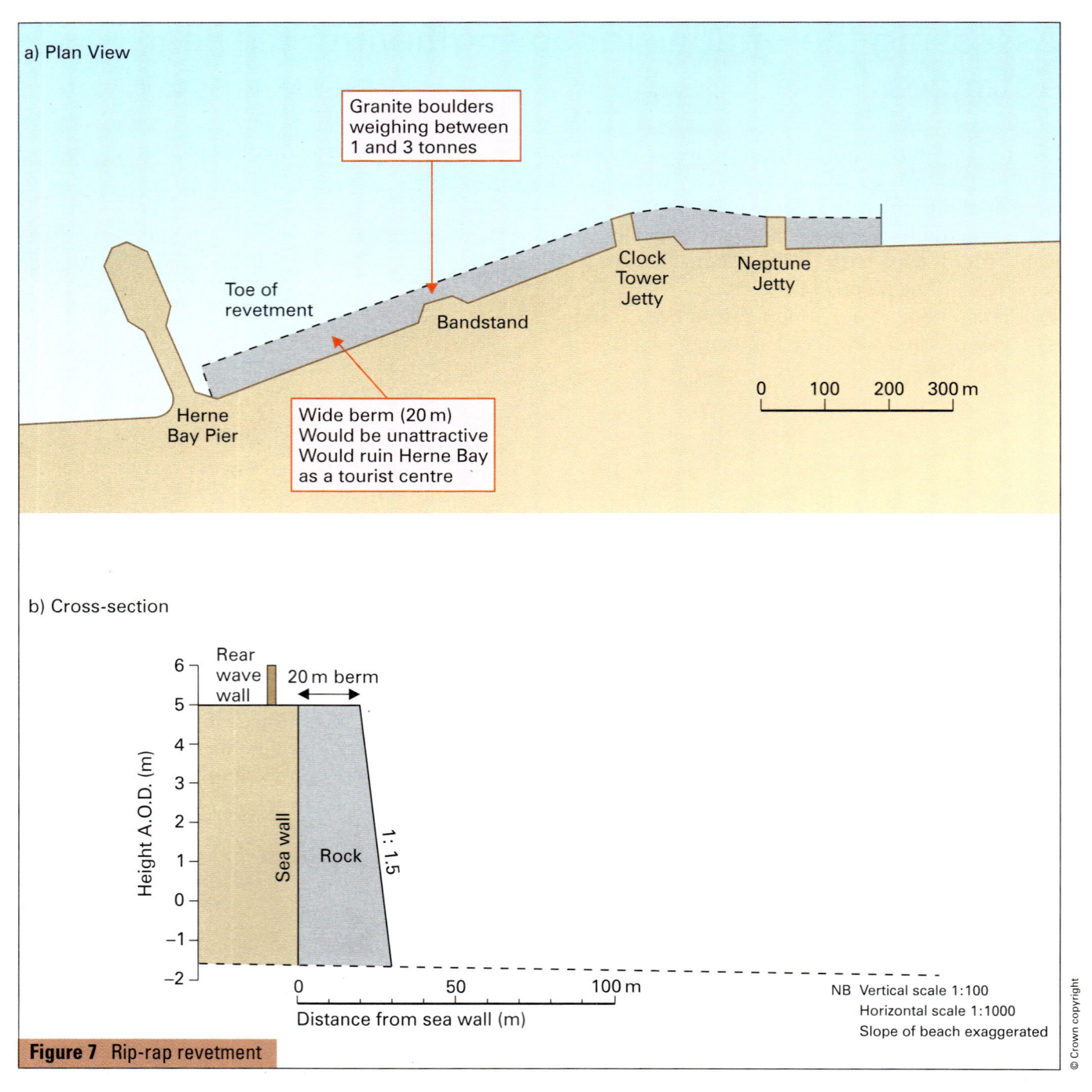

Option 2 viewpoints

The rip-rap might well protect the sea wall and reduce flood risk but I think it will look very ugly.

I think low maintenance costs are an important consideration. Just think how much the Council has been spending on dumping shingle: 5000 tonnes cost £38 000. It was a waste of time and ratepayers' money.

60

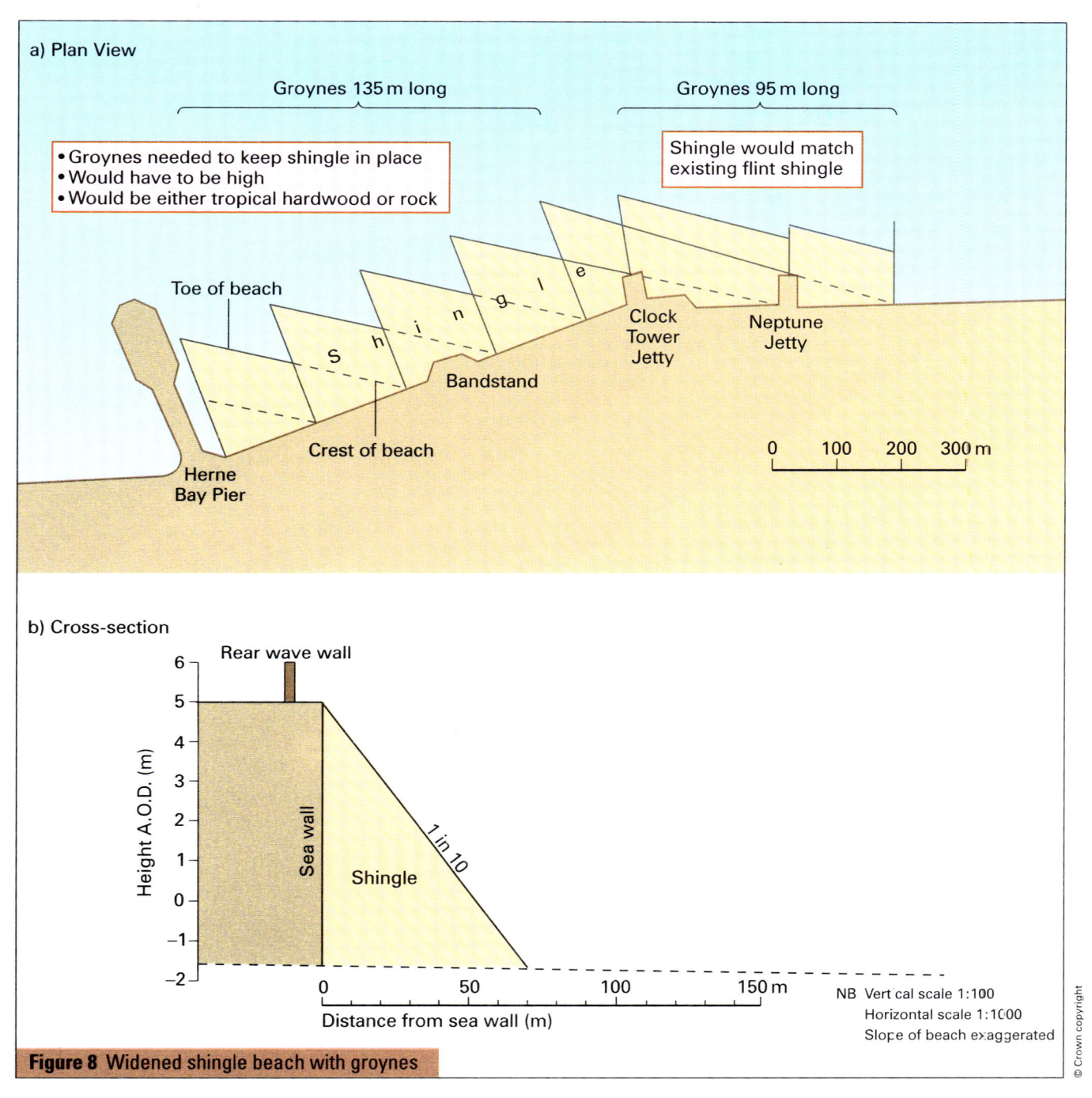

Replacing sea defences in Herne Bay

a) Plan View

Groynes 135 m long | Groynes 95 m long

- Groynes needed to keep shingle in place
- Would have to be high
- Would be either tropical hardwood or rock

Shingle would match existing flint shingle

Toe of beach

Shingle

Clock Tower Jetty
Neptune Jetty
Bandstand
Crest of beach
Herne Bay Pier

0 100 200 300 m

b) Cross-section

Rear wave wall
Sea wall
Shingle
1 in 10

Height A.O.D. (m): -2 to 6
Distance from sea wall (m): 0 to 150 m

NB Vertical scale 1:100
Horizontal scale 1:1000
Slope of beach exaggerated

© Crown copyright

Figure 8 Widened shingle beach with groynes

Option 3 viewpoints

I don't agree with using tropical hardwoods. Deforestation of tropical forests is not environmentally friendly.

I like the idea of retaining our shingle beach but I don't like the look of the groynes needed to keep it in place – they're too long and too high.

Well, if you don't have groynes the beach will disappear after 15 years.

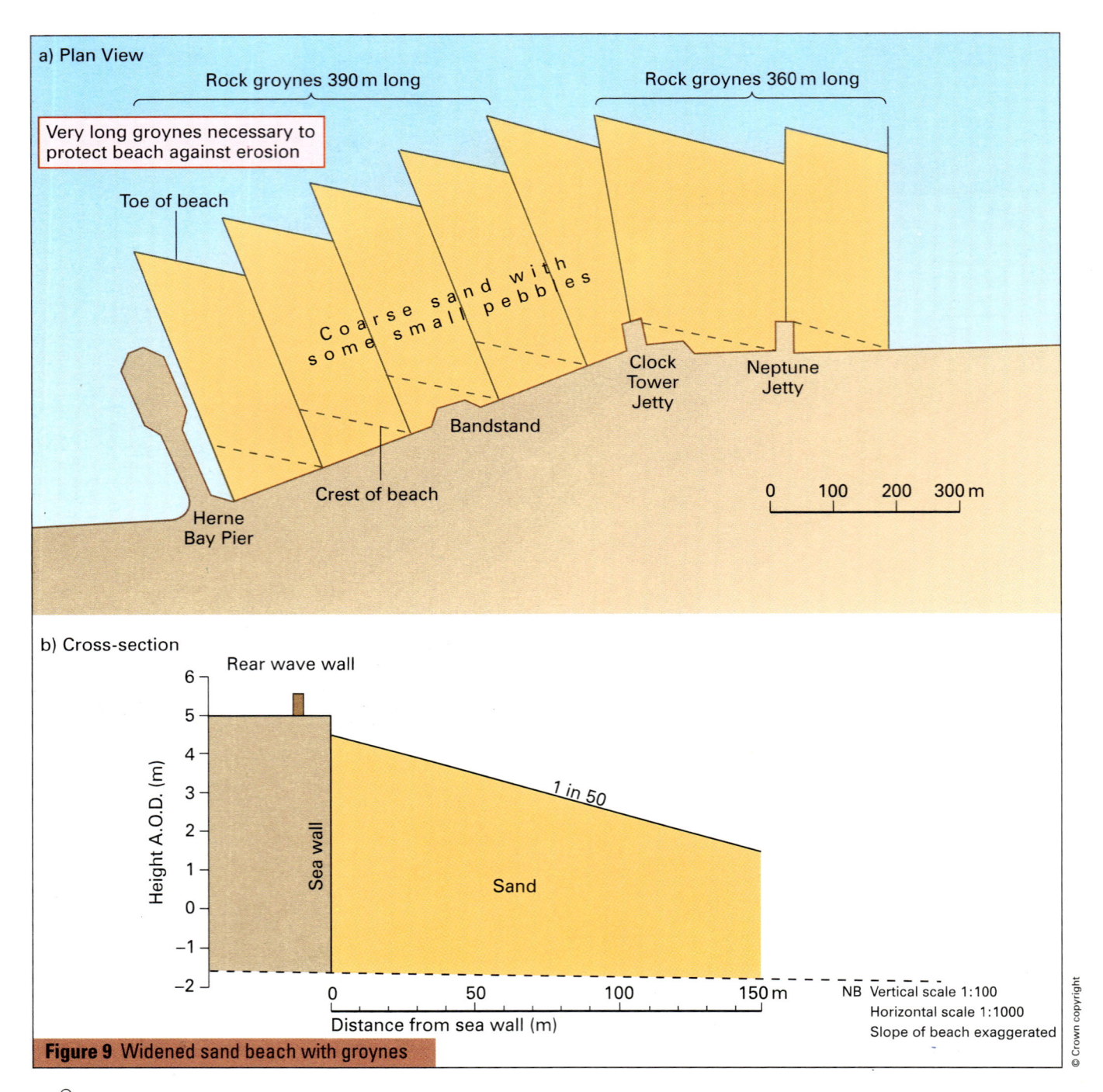

Decision Making Exercises

a) Plan View

Rock groynes 390 m long   Rock groynes 360 m long

Very long groynes necessary to protect beach against erosion

Toe of beach

Coarse sand with some small pebbles

Bandstand
Clock Tower Jetty
Neptune Jetty

Crest of beach

Herne Bay Pier

0   100   200   300 m

b) Cross-section

Rear wave wall

Sea wall

Sand

1 in 50

Height A.O.D. (m)
Distance from sea wall (m)

NB Vertical scale 1:100
Horizontal scale 1:1000
Slope of beach exaggerated

© Crown copyright

Figure 9 Widened sand beach with groynes

Option 4 viewpoints

Well, this option requires even longer groynes and these would have to be rock because timber would be too expensive, and if you didn't have groynes the beach would disappear in 10 years.

I think a sandy beach would be nice for children.

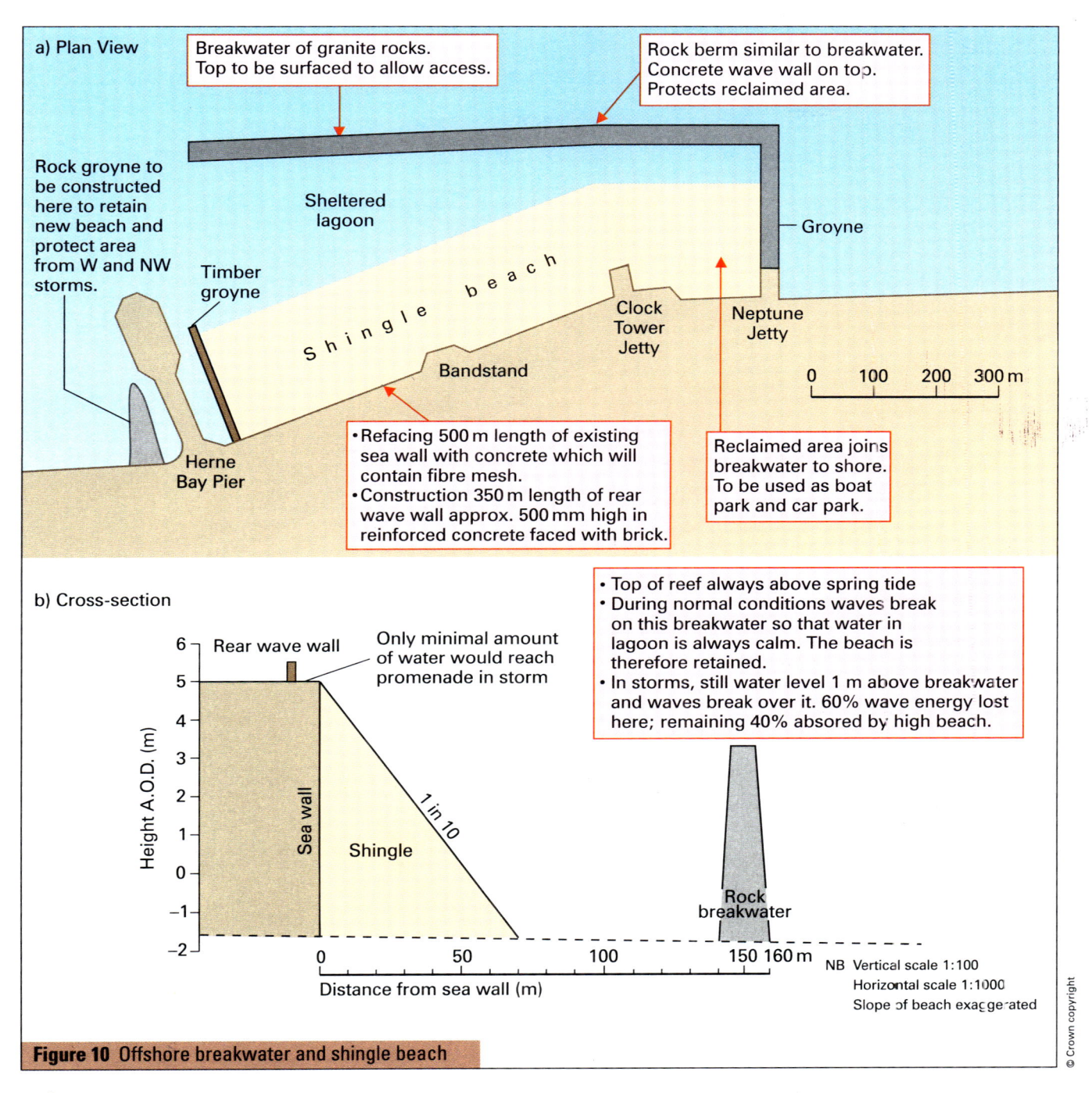

Replacing sea defences in Herne Bay

a) Plan View

- Breakwater of granite rocks. Top to be surfaced to allow access.
- Rock berm similar to breakwater. Concrete wave wall on top. Protects reclaimed area.
- Rock groyne to be constructed here to retain new beach and protect area from W and NW storms.
- Sheltered lagoon
- Timber groyne
- Shingle beach
- Groyne
- Clock Tower Jetty
- Neptune Jetty
- Bandstand
- Herne Bay Pier
- Refacing 500 m length of existing sea wall with concrete which will contain fibre mesh.
- Construction 350 m length of rear wave wall approx. 500 mm high in reinforced concrete faced with brick.
- Reclaimed area joins breakwater to shore. To be used as boat park and car park.

Scale: 0 100 200 300 m

b) Cross-section

- Rear wave wall
- Only minimal amount of water would reach promenade in storm
- Sea wall
- Shingle
- 1 in 10
- Rock breakwater
- Top of reef always above spring tide
- During normal conditions waves break on this breakwater so that water in lagoon is always calm. The beach is therefore retained.
- In storms, still water level 1 m above breakwater and waves break over it. 60% wave energy lost here; remaining 40% absorbed by high beach.

Height A.O.D. (m) axis: −2 to 6
Distance from sea wall (m): 0, 50, 100, 150, 160 m

NB Vertical scale 1:100
Horizontal scale 1:1000
Slope of beach exaggerated

© Crown copyright

Figure 10 Offshore breakwater and shingle beach

Option 5 viewpoints

I think it would be good for people with boats.

I like the offshore breakwater. Herne Bay needs a face lift. The breakwater and marina would be a real focal point for the sea front and would attract lots of visitors. Visitors would bring money into the town.

It looks good but will it really work?

I like the idea of a lower rear wall. The present one is ugly and if you're not on the prom side of it, you can't see the sea.

63

Decision Making Exercises

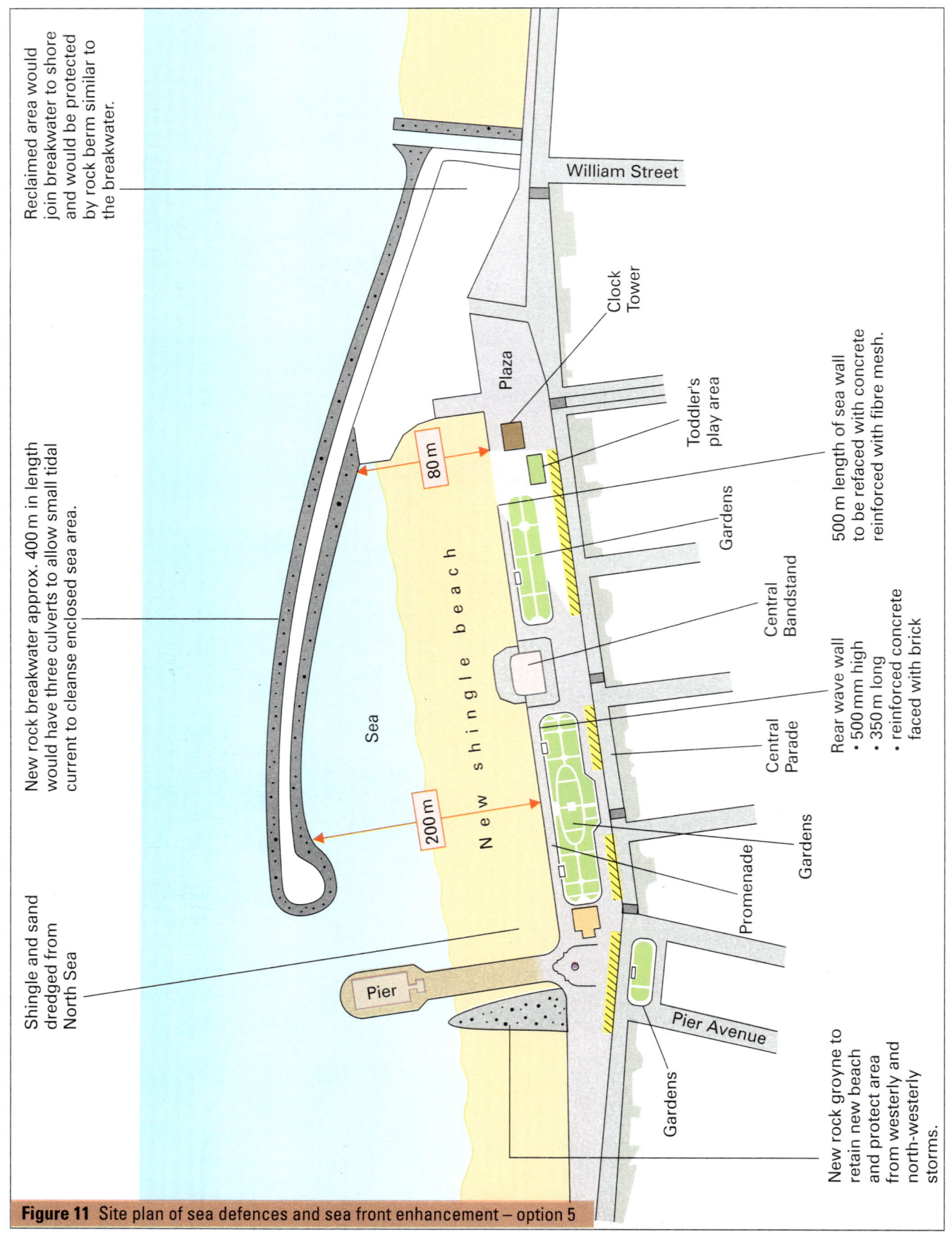

Figure 11 Site plan of sea defences and sea front enhancement – option 5

- Reclaimed area would join breakwater to shore and would be protected by rock berm similar to the breakwater.
- New rock breakwater approx. 400 m in length would have three culverts to allow small tidal current to cleanse enclosed sea area.
- Shingle and sand dredged from North Sea
- New rock groyne to retain new beach and protect area from westerly and north-westerly storms.
- 500 m length of sea wall to be refaced with concrete reinforced with fibre mesh.
- Rear wave wall
  - 500 mm high
  - 350 m long
  - reinforced concrete faced with brick

Labels: William Street, Clock Tower, Plaza, Toddler's play area, Gardens, Central Bandstand, Central Parade, Promenade, Gardens, Pier Avenue, Pier, Sea, New shingle beach

Measurements: 80 m, 200 m

© Crown copyright

Replacing sea defences in Herne Bay

The Decision

Coastal protection works are expensive and most councils have to apply for a government grant from the Ministry of Agriculture, Fisheries and Food. If the nation is paying for the grant (up to 70 per cent of the costs) then clearly it wants to be sure it is getting value for its money. The principal benefits of each scheme were almost identical.

FOUNDATION

1 Draw up a matrix using the following headings:

Scheme	Cost acceptable	Acceptable overtopping rate	Most pleasing environmentally	Most popular with the public

Put ticks in the appropriate boxes to help you decide which option is the best.

2 a) State which option you think is best.
  b) Give three reasons for your choice.

HIGHER

1 a) Using all available evidence throughout the study, decide which option you think is best value.
  b) State clearly the reasons for your choice.
2 For *one* of the other options give reasons why you rejected it.

Summary

Herne Bay has a long history of coastal erosion and flooding. Despite attempts to maintain a protective beach by a system of groynes and by dumping shingle, longshore drift and the lack of natural replenishment rendered this task a losing battle. The sea wall thus was subjected to the destructive action of the waves. In addition, the sea wall was old, and was not sufficiently high enough to provide satisfactory protection against a storm as severe as that experienced in 1953. New sea defences were essential to protect the sea wall and to reduce overtopping and consequent flooding of the town. Canterbury City Council was determined to select the scheme which would give the best value for money and also be environmentally attractive. Research had shown that new works could attract 13 per cent more visitors and boost Herne Bay's role as a resort.

Glossary

berm narrow artificial ridge or ledge which acts as part of the sea defences; similar to breakwater

longshore drift movement of material along a beach by wave action

North Sea surge rapid rise in sea level caused by a deep atmospheric depression

7 Should permission be given for a wind farm on Gunson Height?

Background information

Since the **commissioning** of Delabole wind farm in November 1991, wind farms (clusters of wind turbines) are becoming a more common feature of the landscape in upland rural areas of north and west Britain.

Wind energy has been harnessed by humans for more than 2000 years. Windmills were used to provide mechanical energy but became obsolete by the end of the nineteenth century. Attention has once more been focused on wind power, but now with the object of generating electricity.

Since the 1970s several factors have led to the development of wind power. It was triggered by the Middle East oil crisis in 1973 which resulted in price increases in oil. Growing demands for electricity, as it plays an increasingly important role in our lives, have made us aware of the fact that we must not rely on non-renewable resources.

Figure 1 Location of Gunson Height and Kirkby Moor wind farms

Priorities for electricity generation

At present most of our electricity is generated from fossil fuels – coal, oil and natural gas. A further 25 per cent is from nuclear energy dependent on supplies of uranium. **Sustainable development** is a priority, and so is environmental protection. Growing awareness of environmental damage caused by burning fuels and the hazards associated with nuclear power generation and disposal of nuclear waste are further considerations.

Lastly, political crises such as the Gulf War (1991) reinforce the fact that our fuel supplies are not necessarily secure.

Wind energy is one of the most promising sources of renewable energy, but even this source of electricity is not without its drawbacks. Visual impact and noise are both sensitive issues, as this study will illustrate.

---

1 List the fossil fuels used for the generation of electricity.
2 Why are environmental protection and sustainable development now top priorities in the production of energy?
3 What are the drawbacks of wind energy?
4 Suggest why upland areas of west and north Britain provide the best sites for wind farms.

Should permission be given for a wind farm on Gunson Height?

The need for wind power

A It makes ENVIRONMENTAL SENSE

- All forms of energy production have an environmental impact, but that from wind power is low, local and manageable.
- Wind power is:
    - safe – no hazardous waste
    - non-polluting
      – no global warming (no carbon dioxide)
      – no acid rain (no sulphur dioxide or nitrogen oxides)
    - abundant
    - sustainable (renewable).
- Turbines can easily be removed at the end of their life (25 years) and the site returned to its original use.

B It makes ECONOMIC SENSE

- Wind power is a cost-effective source of energy that:
    - compares favourably with new coal-fired stations
    - is cheaper than nuclear power
    - costs only 4.32p/kWh in England and Wales.
- Wind power can create employment and income for the local community during installation, but more importantly in running and maintenance – very important in rural areas where the need for alternative jobs is essential.
- It can increase the income of the farmer on whose land the wind farm is sited.

C It makes STRATEGIC SENSE

- Because wind farms are spread over a number of locations within the distribution network of regional companies, they generate electricity nearer to their consumers. This cuts down the loss of electricity through transmission.
- Power generation is well matched to the season of greatest demand – winter. Winds are strong at this time of year.
- Wind power can benefit island communities exposed to strong winds. Often isolation means that the only other choice of generating electricity is by diesel fuel, expensive to import. It would be ideal, therefore, to combine wind power with the existing diesel system.

Decision Making Exercises

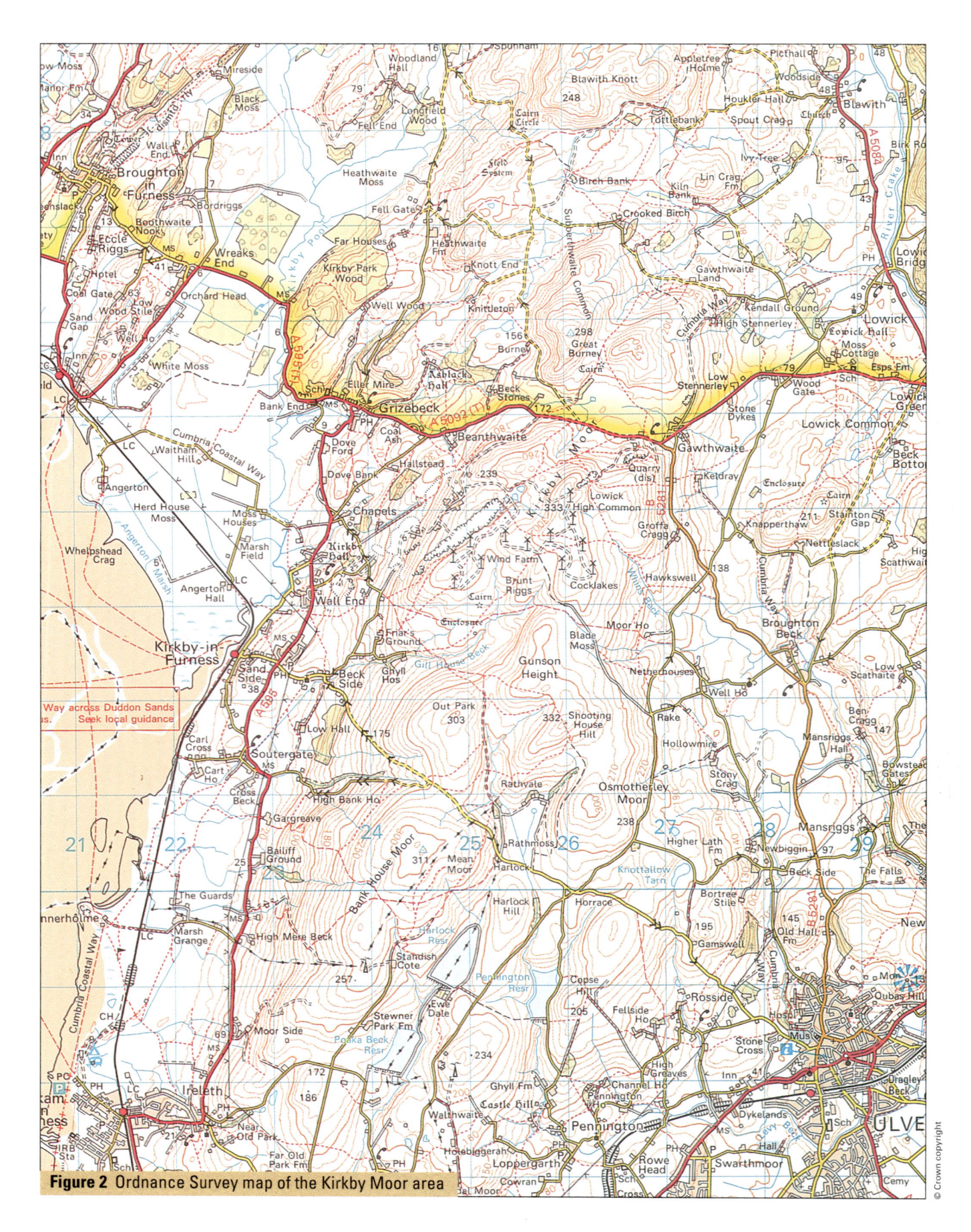

Figure 2 Ordnance Survey map of the Kirkby Moor area

Should permission be given for a wind farm on Gunson Height?

Kirkby Moor wind farm

Figure 3a Kirkby Moor – site of wind farm prior to its construction

Figure 3b Kirkby Moor wind farm

Study Figure 2, the Ordnance Survey Landranger 96 1:50 000 (2 cm to 1 km) map extract, Figures 3a and 3b, and the information boxes on page 67 to help you assess the area in terms of a) its environmental value, and b) the impact of the wind farm on the environment by answering the questions below.

Kirkby Moor is part of a ridge of hills extending south from the centre of the Lake District. Coniston Old Man, 13 km to the north, is also on this ridge. Barrow-in-Furness, the largest settlement (71 900), is 15 km distant. The Duddon estuary (sandy area in the west) is an important wintering habitat for wildfowl and waders.

Site
1. Using the OS map (Fig. 2) and Figures 3a and 3b, describe the area.
2. a) Above what height are the wind turbines?
   b) How does this compare with other summits in this area? Why is altitude an important factor?
   c) Describe the slope of the site.
3. Winds have a westerly component. Suggest why this is a good site.
4. How accessible is the site for construction and maintenance crews?
5. a) Which is the nearest large settlement?
   b) How far away is the nearest point on the electricity transmission line?

Environmental impact
6. What activity has already disfigured the landscape?
7. How near is the Lake District National Park to the turbines a) nearest, b) furthest from its southern boundary?
8. a) What impact do you think the wind farms will have on views from nearby summits?
   b) How many turbines are there?
   c) Looking at Figure 3b, how intrusive are the turbines?

Local benefits
9. Suggest how the local community might benefit from the wind farm.

Decision Making Exercises

Points of view

Read the views expressed on this page. Which views agree with your own?

> These wind turbines are massive features, 24 m high. They're about 250 m apart so they're quite spread out.

ENVIRONMENTAL GROUP SPOKESPERSON

> We need wind farms to cut down on pollution. Kirkby Moor saves 12 000 tonnes of carbon dioxide and 130 tonnes of acid rain gases a year. These early wind farms are important. By assessing their performance we can judge their efficiency and make improvements for the future.

POWER COMPANY MANAGER

> I'm in favour of wind farms but not here! Mind you, they tell me that 82 per cent of the residents support the development of wind farms in the area.

RESIDENT

> Wind turbines are no worse than electricity pylons or telecommunication towers. They, in fact, occupy only 1.5 per cent of the wind farm. The electricity generated is taken by underground cable to a substation so really there is the minimum of visual pollution.

WORKER FOR A POWER COMPANY

> We feel Burlington slate quarry on the north-western side of Kirkby Moor is in harmony with the landscape, but these turbines can be seen from a wide range of viewpoints up to 8 km away. From Great Burney – a popular low-level walk – they are assertive and contrast starkly with the heather.

LOCAL AUTHORITY PLANNER

> Kirkby Moor is an **SSSI** noted in particular for its heather. Construction of the wind farm will not only damage the heather but some will be lost.

NATURE GROUP MEMBER

Should permission be given for a wind farm on Gunson Height?

The problem

The nation urgently needs wind energy but unfortunately wind turbines are seen by some to be a symbol of visual pollution, disfiguring the environment. While the need for 'green' energy is great, the extension of Kirkby Moor wind farm on to Gunson Height would, in the opinion of many, have too great a visual impact. There are several other wind farms nearby, for example on Harlock Hill, and two other projects are in the pipeline (Fig. 4). It is feared by landscape conservationists that the Furness peninsula could become the wind power capital of England. Should planning permission be granted for Gunson Height?

As with Kirkby Moor, a public inquiry took place. It was held at Ulverston in February 1997. It was hoped by the conservationists, who fear that the boundary of the Lake District National Park could be fringed with wind turbines, that National Wind Power would not win their appeal against the South Lake District Council which had refused planning permission. In the case of Kirkby Moor the Secretary of State decided that the need for the development of green energy outweighed any harm that might be caused by the visual impact of the wind turbines. Planning policies for the area are against new developments unless they are essential for the needs of agriculture or forestry, or if social and economic benefits outweigh environmental costs.

Kirkby Moor wind farm: fact file

- occupies 150 hectares of moorland
- generates enough electricity for 4000 homes (Ulverston has 4750 households)
- helps to satisfy the need for extra power locally
- would need shorter overhead line than any alternative source would require and transmission losses would be reduced
- located about 800 m from nearest dwellings: noise level 40 **dBA**.

Wind farm	Number of turbines	Homes served/year	Start date
Haverigg (coastal, disused airfield W. of Millom)	5	704	Aug 1992
Kirksanton (coastal, disused airfield W. of Millom)	4	1865	–
Kirkby Moor	12	3003	Sept 1993
Harlock Hill (near KM)	5	1564	Jan 1997
Siddick (coastal, near Workington, on reclaimed site of old coal workings)	7	2609	Aug 1996
Oldside (next to Siddick)	9	3354	Aug 1996
Great Orton (6 km W. of Carlisle)	10	1877	Jan 1993

Figure 4 Cumbria wind farms

Decision Making Exercises

Assessing the three options

Option 1 – Develop Gunson Height

- This option would increase the output of green energy, supplying enough electricity for the needs of a further 7000 homes.
- It would cut down on harmful emissions of sulphur and nitrogen oxides which cause acid rain. This, in turn, causes damage to moorland, trees and rivers.
- Development of Gunson Height would mean more than doubling the number of turbines in a very small area.
- Many feel that the small amount of energy generated does not justify the visual impact on the landscape. Environmentally, the area is similar to Kirkby Moor.

Figure 5 A wind turbine at Anglesey, Wales: this photograph gives you some idea of the scale of these features

Should permission be given for a wind farm on Gunson Height?

2 Option 2 – Not develop Gunson Height but develop alternative sites elsewhere in Furness

- Visual impact and noise pollution are drawbacks present wherever wind farms are located. Noise levels can be compared with those of a car 600 m away travelling at 40 mph.

- Although coastal sites provide alternative locations, wind strength at lower altitudes is less and, therefore, more turbines are required so putting up costs.

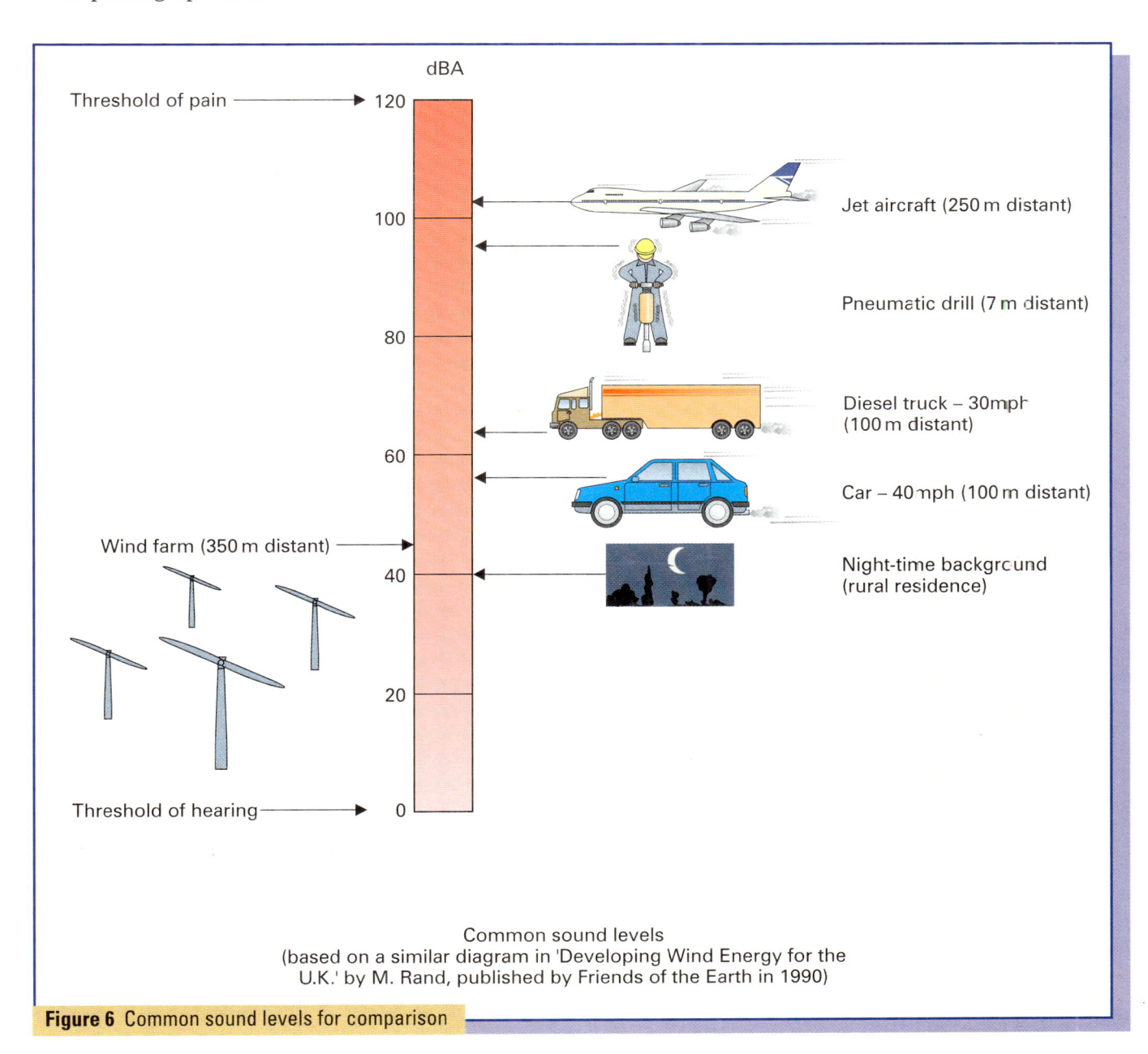

dBA

- Threshold of pain — 120
- Jet aircraft (250 m distant) — 100
- Pneumatic drill (7 m distant) — ~95
- 80
- Diesel truck – 30 mph (100 m distant) — ~65
- 60
- Car – 40 mph (100 m distant) — ~55
- Wind farm (350 m distant) — ~40
- Night-time background (rural residence) — ~40
- 20
- Threshold of hearing — 0

Common sound levels
(based on a similar diagram in 'Developing Wind Energy for the U.K.' by M. Rand, published by Friends of the Earth in 1990)

Figure 6 Common sound levels for comparison

Decision Making Exercises

Option 3 – No further developments in the Furness peninsula

- While the environment would be safeguarded from visual and noise pollution and ecological disturbance, the local economy will suffer from loss of the income which could be gained during the construction period.
- On completion a wind farm would provide two to three full-time jobs for qualified technicians.
- Wind farms also provide a boost to the economy of the local community:

  • cost of rents and maintenance on a typical wind farm can mean that a power company may contribute in the order of £150 000 a year to the local economy.

  • funds established by power companies provide for a variety of benefits for the local community: student sponsorships; equipment for schools; repairs to village halls.

- All these factors help to maintain the viability of the community and so help reduce rural depopulation.

Figure 7 Burlington slate quarry: some people consider that the slate quarry greatly disfigures the landscape

Should permission be given for a wind farm on Gunson Height?

The Decision

FOUNDATION

1 Draw up a table with six headings: Option number; Visual impact; Noise pollution; Other environmental harm; Cost; Local benefits. Fill in the columns for each option.
2 Using the information in your table decide whether or not the wind farm at Gunson Height should be developed. Give three reasons to explain your decision.

HIGHER

1 Choose which option you think is preferable. Give reasons for your choice.
2 For one of the other options give reasons why you think it unsatisfactory.

Summary

Decisions regarding wind farms are difficult to make in terms of environmental considerations. On the one hand, wind power is green energy, but, on the other hand, wind turbines themselves can be regarded as visual pollution of the environment. Suitable sites are frequently areas of great landscape value where the public hope to escape from the trappings of modern civilisation. Our other priority is sustainable development. 'Wind power is clean, renewable and efficient.' (National Wind Power)

Glossary

commissioning starting up production

dBA decibel (dB) scale A: measurement of sound (40 dBA is the equivalent of night-time background noise for a rural area)

SSSI Site of Special Scientific Interest

sustainable development development which considers the needs of future generations

8 Improving the approach road to Ramsgate Harbour (Port Ramsgate)

Background information

Ramsgate in the Isle of Thanet, East Kent, has always been an important gateway to mainland Europe (Fig. 1); in fact, there was a port at Ramsgate in Roman times. Only since the early 1970s, however, has Ramsgate developed into one of the main cross-Channel ports.

The construction of the M25 in the 1970s and its link with the M2 has provided Ramsgate with good access to the UK motorway system. The Thanet Way is the direct link to the port and was constructed in the 1930s, largely to help speed holidaymakers to and from the Thanet resorts. Until recently, the Thanet Way has been increasingly congested. However, much of this road has now been widened to dual carriageway and the remaining section is due for completion within the next few years. This will improve access to Ramsgate which, in turn, will encourage the rapid expansion of the port.

Figure 1 Location of Ramsgate Harbour

The history of Port Ramsgate

1749	Construction of the main harbour begins.
1791	Harbour completed.
1966	The world's first public hovercraft service begins operating from the harbour. The inner harbour becomes a marina.
1980	Land reclaimed west of the Royal Harbour ready for a cross-Channel ferry service.
1981	The Sally Line begins a combined passenger and freight service to Dunkerque.
1983	A freight service to Oostende begins.
1984	A £1.2 million breakwater is put in place to protect the port's increasing traffic from bad weather all year round. More land is reclaimed.
1985	A deeper approach channel is dredged.
1990	More land is reclaimed to enlarge port facilities.
1991	A passenger reception area is redeveloped.
1994	The Dover–Oostende service is transferred to Ramsgate, so traffic is increased by over 50 per cent. To allow for this development, £6 million is spent on dredging, piling and major berth additions and modifications.

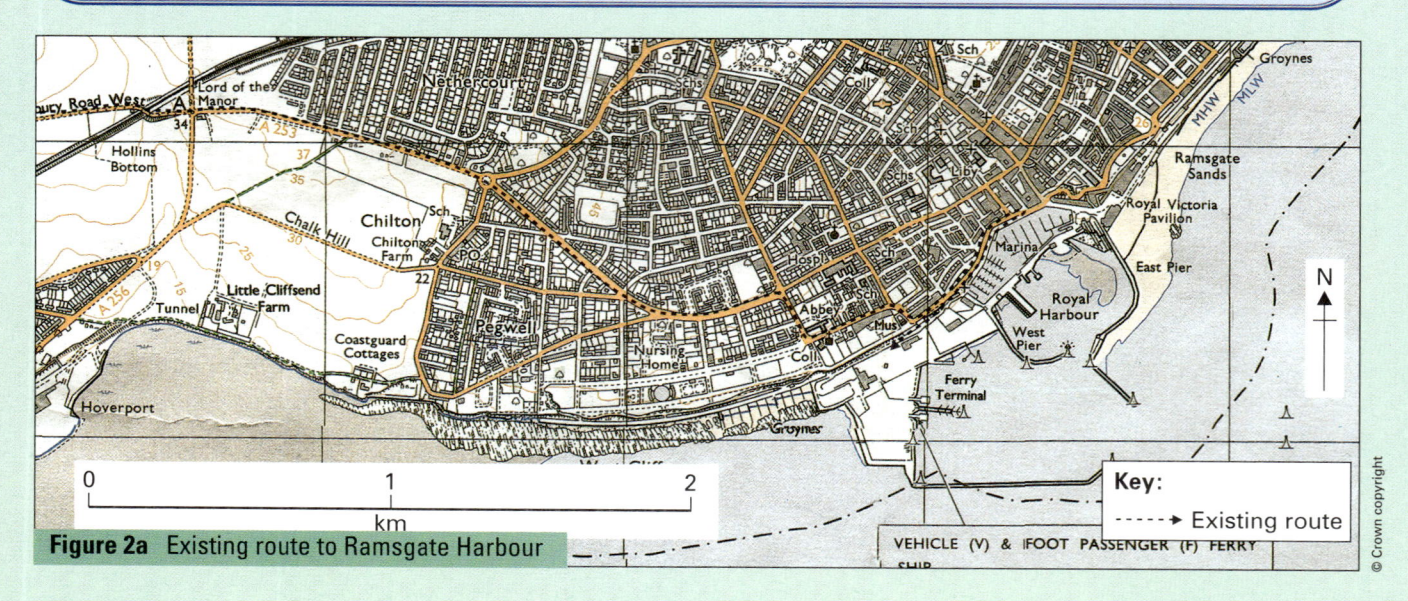

Figure 2a Existing route to Ramsgate Harbour

Key:
- - - - → Existing route

Improving the approach road to Ramsgate Harbour

Figure 2b Aerial view of Port Ramsgate

The future of Port Ramsgate

The port is destined to grow into the twenty-first century. More than £32 million has already been invested. Plans for improvement include:
- double-deck vehicle ramps
- floating terminal for Jetfoils
- deeper approach tunnel
- moving the present breakwater further south to allow ships a larger turning circle
- new Jetfoil terminal with departure lounge, customs facilities and duty-free shop.

	Passengers	Cars	Coaches	Freight
1981	132 120	16 000	105	1000
1982	431 583	57 222	2295	7305
1983	602 854	63 782	3316	18 565
1984	663 250	88 404	4256	63 088
1985	1 002 702	126 003	7777	77 362
1986	1 218 312	132 167	10 850	77 710
1987	1 255 030	134 920	10 634	96 200
1988	1 571 414	185 483	15 279	121 588
1989	1 485 352	175 951	14 256	153 715
1990	1 517 358	154 228	15 887	163 657
1991	1 739 321	212 882	16 230	176 156
1992	1 872 089	253 698	16 616	201 014
1993	1 992 942	262 436	14 134	211 902
1994	3 583 835	473 405	20 768	261 079
1995	3 392 192	499 197	19 192	235 654
TOTAL	22 460 354	2 835 778	171 595	1 865 995

Figure 3 Port Ramsgate traffic 1981–95

1. a) Give four reasons why Ramsgate has developed into an important cross-Channel port.
   b) Suggest why the port did not really expand before the 1970s.
2. Using the map (Fig. 2a) and the aerial photograph (Fig. 2b), draw a labelled sketch of the harbour/port area to show: the Royal Harbour; the cliffs; the marina; the ferry terminal piers; the new harbour walls; the port terminal buildings and the freight parking area.
3. Study the statistics (Fig. 3) which show the increase of traffic through the port between 1981 and 1995.
   a) Construct a graph to show this increase for one of the categories given.
   b) Between which two years was the greatest increase in traffic?
   c) Suggest one reason for this increase.
   d) What evidence suggests that improved access to the port is needed?

Decision Making Exercises

The existing situation – why a new approach road to the port is needed

Figure 4 London Road

Steep gradient causes traffic queues behind slow-moving vehicles. Noise pollution is another problem in this residential area.

Saxon Road
Goodwin Road
London Road to Port Ramsgate

- the main route to the port follows the A253, Canterbury Road East and the B2054.
- The B2054 passes through the residential roads of London Road (Fig. 4), Grange Road, St Augustine's Road (Fig. 5), the Paragon (Fig. 7) and Royal Parade (Fig. 8).
- The residential roads are unsuitable for heavy goods vehicles.
- In many places, the roads are narrow with buildings close to the edge of the road.

Church – listed building
St Augustine's Abbey – listed building
St Augustine's Road

Figure 5 St Augustine's Road

Improving the approach road to Ramsgate Harbour

- At the Paragon corner and at the small roundabout by the harbour, heavy goods vehicles need to use the whole road width for turning.
- The present route has poor visibility and numerous side junctions.
- The steep gradients on Royal Parade and London Road cause traffic queues behind slow-moving vehicles.
- The central area of Ramsgate is an important conservation area – at the present time, heavy goods vehicles have to pass through the area.

Figure 6 Road traffic impact and the physical conditions on the existing route to the harbour

	Road traffic impacts				Physical conditions		
Sections	Noise	Visual intrusion	Pedestrian/ traffic conflict	Potential for congestion	Gradient	Proximity of properties to road	Road alignment
Canterbury Road East							
London Road (West)							
London Road (East)							
Grange Road							
St Augustine's Road							
The Paragon							
Royal Parade							
Military Road							

Key: ☐ Very significant ☐ Negligible ☐ Very poor ☐ Neutral/(good)
     ☐ Significant   ☐ Poor

Figure 7 The Paragon

- 90° bend forces lorries to use both sides of the road when turning
- Hotels and guest houses suffer noise and visual pollution
- Cliff-top promenade overlooking harbour
- Pavement
- 90° bend

Figure 8 Royal Parade

- Hotels, guesthouses, holiday apartments suffer noise and visual pollution
- Steep gradient – increased noise pollution from lorries braking or labouring up the slope
- Military Road – narrow road leading to Port Ramsgate
- Lorries in conflict with tourist area of harbour
- Pleasure craft in Marina

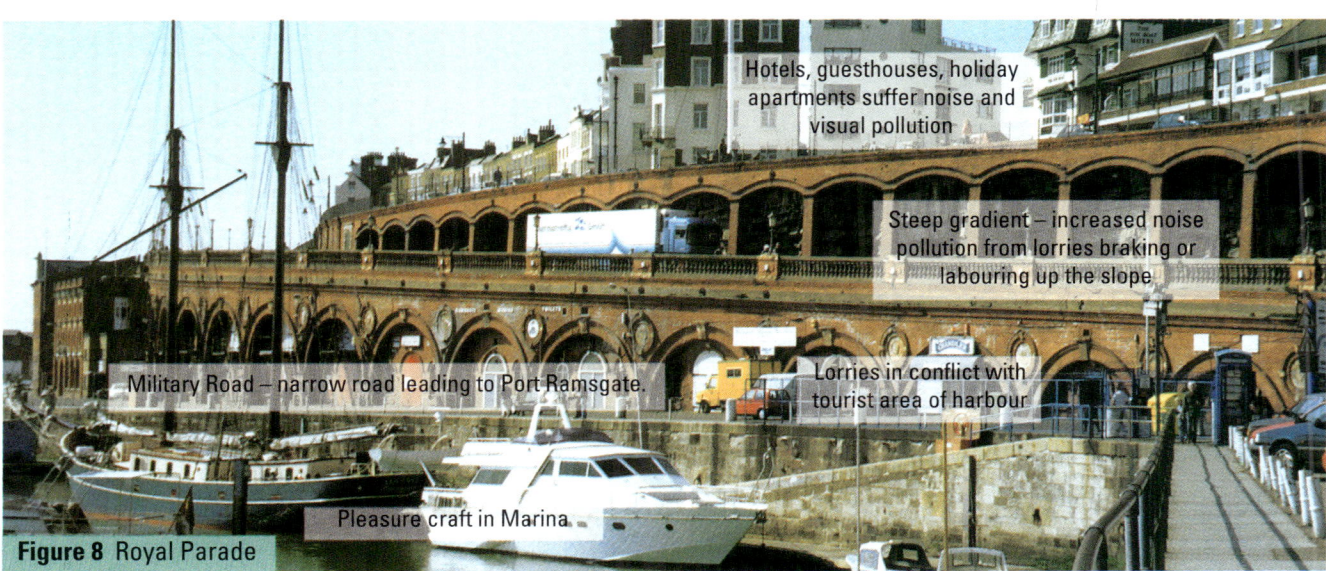

Decision Making Exercises

Figure 9 Royal Parade and Military Road

Hotels, guesthouses
To Port Ramsgate
Military Road
Marina Resort Hotel

Mini roundabout at junction of Royal Parade and Military Road was too small for heavy goods vehicles to drive round

- The removal of heavy traffic from the conservation area would increase the scope for improved leisure and tourist activity.

- The port itself would benefit from improved access.

FOUNDATION

4 a) What is meant by the term 'conservation area'?
b) Using the information given in Figure 6 and the photographs taken along the existing route, give four disadvantages of the present route to the harbour.

HIGHER

4 Using all the information given, explain the disadvantages of the present route to the harbour from the point of view of: a) a lorry driver, b) a resident who lives in St Augustine's Road.

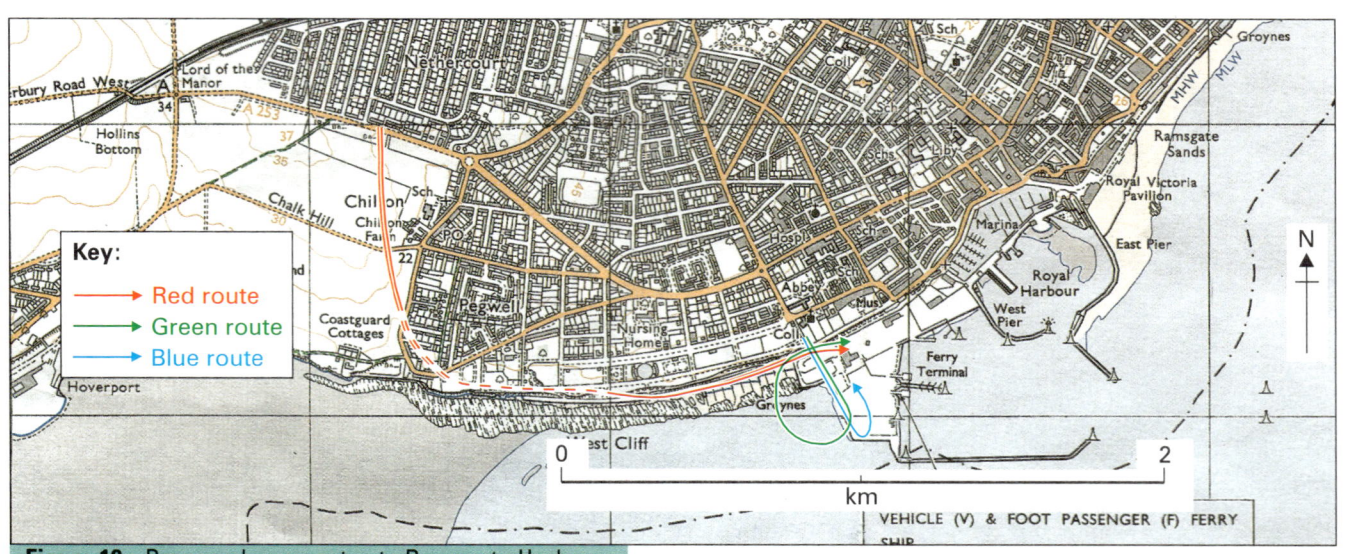

Key:
→ Red route
→ Green route
→ Blue route

Figure 10 Proposed new routes to Ramsgate Harbour

Possible options for a new approach road to the harbour

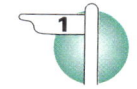

Option 1 (Red Route)

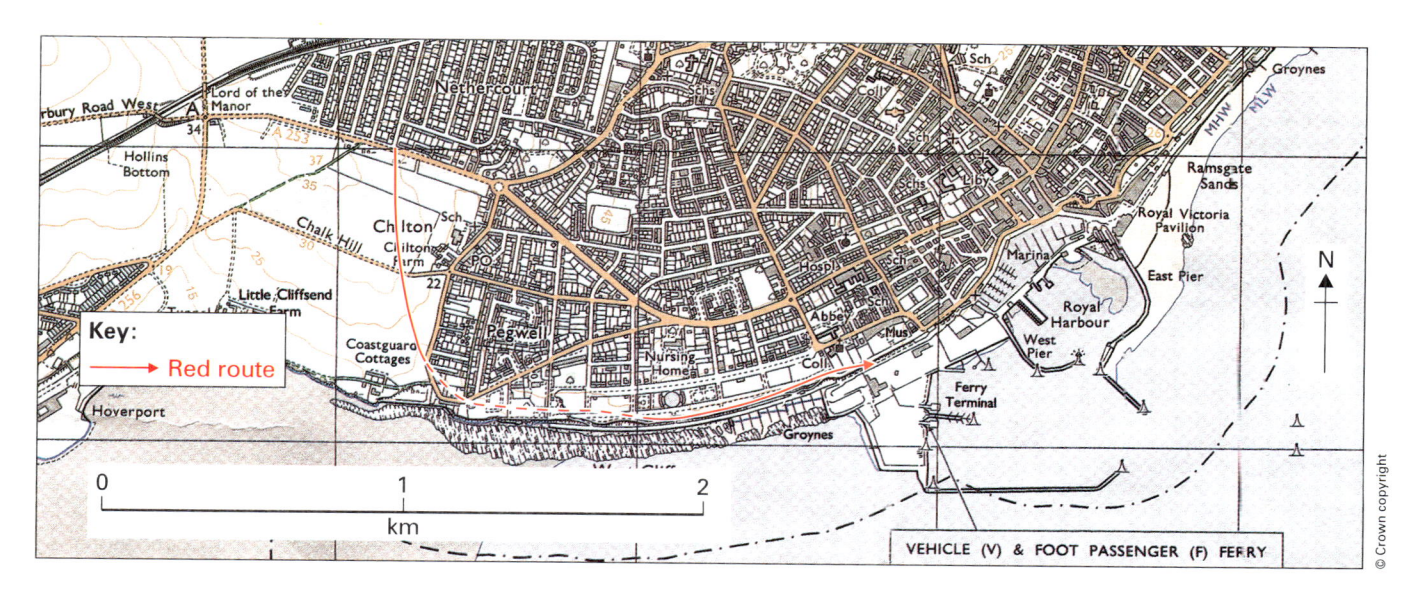

A new road heading south from a new roundabout on the A253 would cut across an area of allotments and farmland to the west of the urban area. The road would then go into a tunnel (215 m of cut-and-cover tunnel and 475 m of bored tunnel) under Pegwell to emerge on the Western Undercliff which it would then follow to the harbour.

Decision Making Exercises

Option 2 (Green Route)

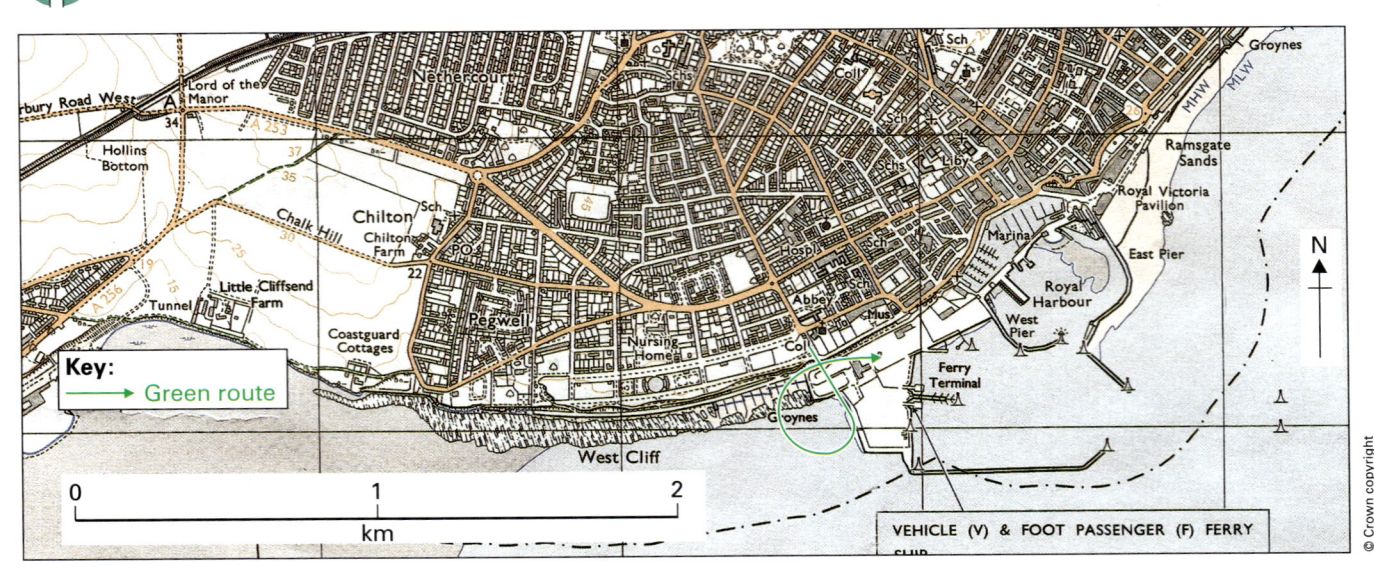

A spiral ramp. A new road would begin at the southern end of Grange Road and run out over the port in an elevated section. It would then spiral downhill, in a clockwise direction and pass out over the sea to join the Western Undercliff at the west of the ferry port.

Improving the approach road to Ramsgate Harbour

Option 3 (Blue Route)

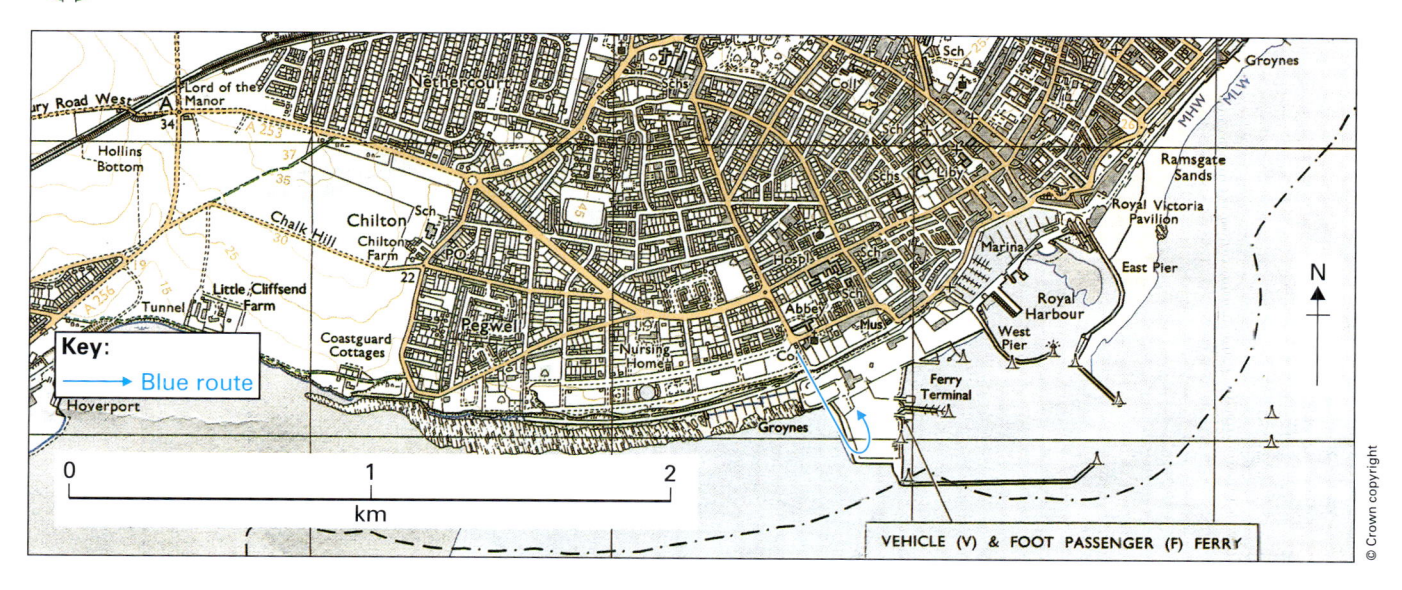

A straight ramp. A new road would begin at the southern end of Grange Road and continue as a straight ramp to a roundabout at the south-western corner of the ferry port. A surface road would then bring traffic back to the Undercliff area.

Environmental assessment of the three options

The Red Route

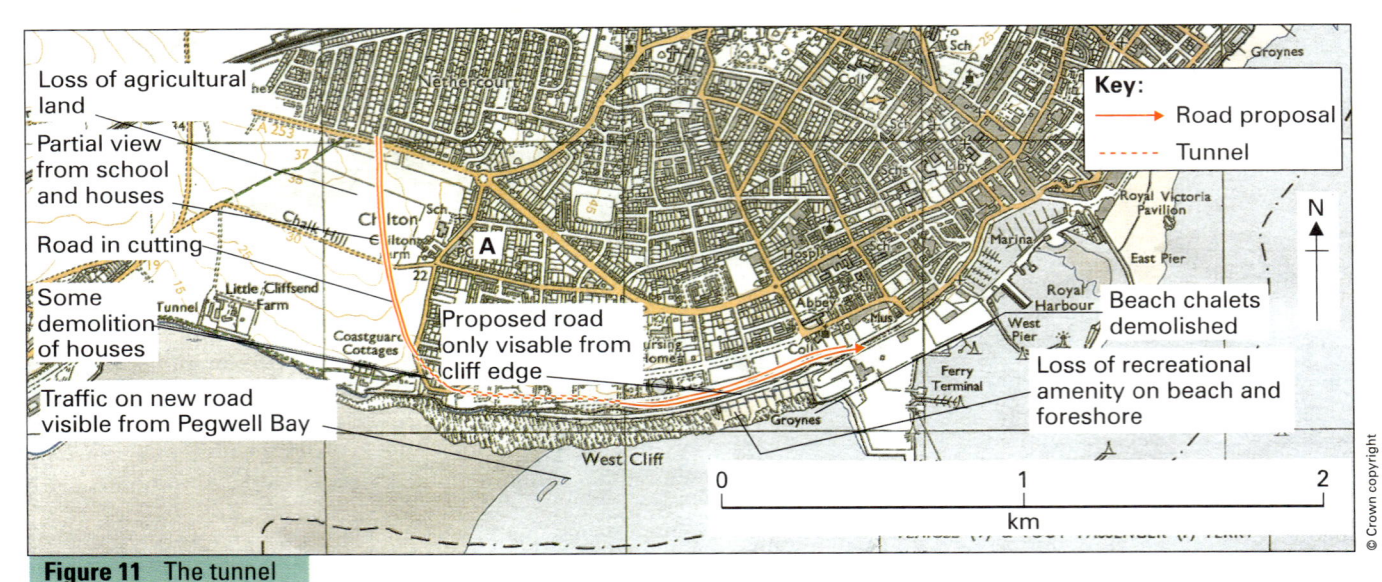

Figure 11 The tunnel

Map labels:
- Loss of agricultural land
- Partial view from school and houses
- Road in cutting
- Some demolition of houses
- Traffic on new road visible from Pegwell Bay
- Proposed road only visible from cliff edge
- Beach chalets demolished
- Loss of recreational amenity on beach and foreshore

Key:
- Road proposal
- Tunnel

- Ten properties would need to be demolished.
- Some limited damage may occur to listed buildings in Pegwell during tunnelling.
- Existing open land to the immediate west of the urban area would be affected by traffic.
- The view along the coast could be affected by the traffic along the Undercliff road. At present, the Undercliff is used for recreational purposes such as walking and fishing. Although these activities could continue after road construction, they would be greatly affected by traffic.
- The cliffs at the Undercliff (part of the Sandwich Bay SSSI) would be greatly affected by the tunnel entrance.
- Although, for part of the route, traffic noise and vibration would be limited due to the use of the tunnel, residential areas on the western edge of the urban area and the Undercliff would be affected.
- The Undercliff walk would be less attractive to pedestrians.
- Air quality may improve due to traffic increasing in speed.

FOUNDATION

5 Locate the area on the map (Fig. 11) shown by letter A.
a) Why might some people living in the area be in favour of the Red Route?
b) Why might others living in the same area be against the Red Route?

Improving the approach road to Ramsgate Harbour

The Green Route

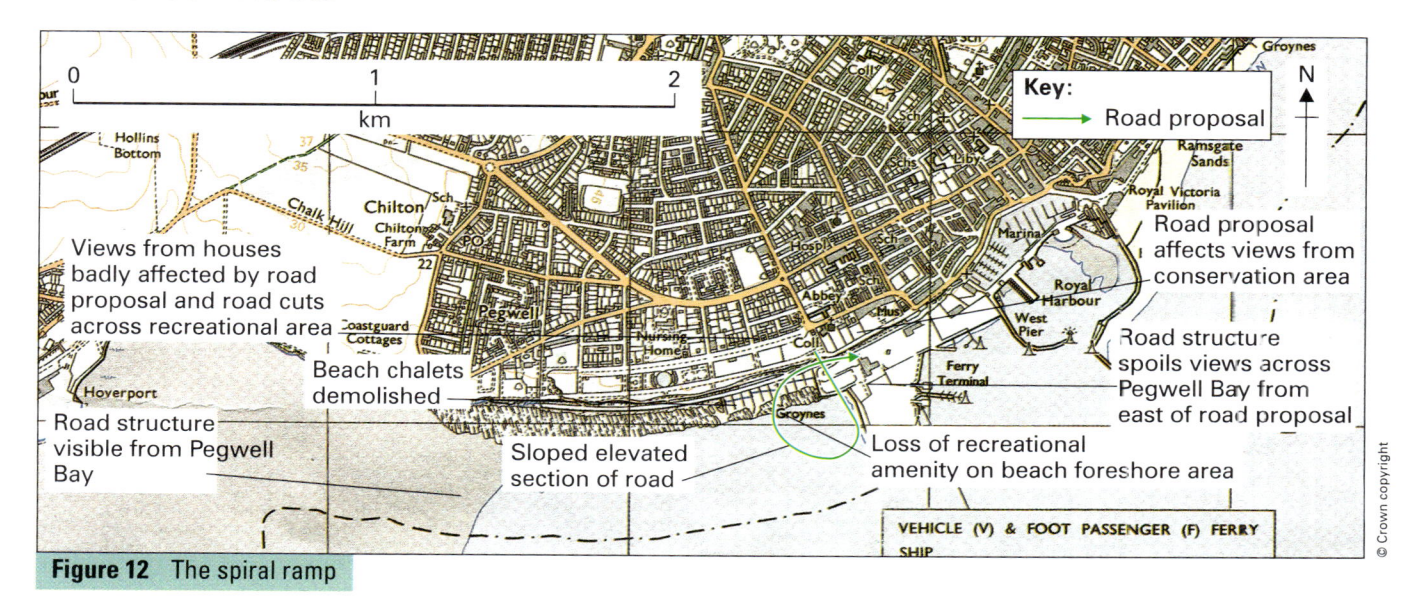

Figure 12 The spiral ramp

- During construction of the route, the cement lorries would increase the level of traffic and there would be disruption to pedestrian movements along the Promenade.
- Older buildings such as The Grange (a Grade 1 listed building) could be affected by increased traffic along the new route.
- The route would have a significant impact on the foreshore and the intertidal zone (three supports would be tied to the intertidal zone and five on the seabed below low water). This wavecut platform is within the SSSI of Sandwich Bay.
- The road would cut across the relatively unspoilt view of Pegwell Bay and cliffs, thus causing visual pollution when viewed from the east.
- The elevated section could produce high noise levels which would be impossible to screen, although it would be against background port and sea noise.
- As the route is shorter than the existing one, there would be an overall reduction in air pollution.
- Road users would have the advantage of a direct route, but the elevated section may need to be closed during periods of severe weather, particularly to high-sided vehicles.

HIGHER

5 a) What is meant by the term 'SSSI'?
b) Explain how the new road may conflict with the SSSI.

Decision Making Exercises

The Blue Route

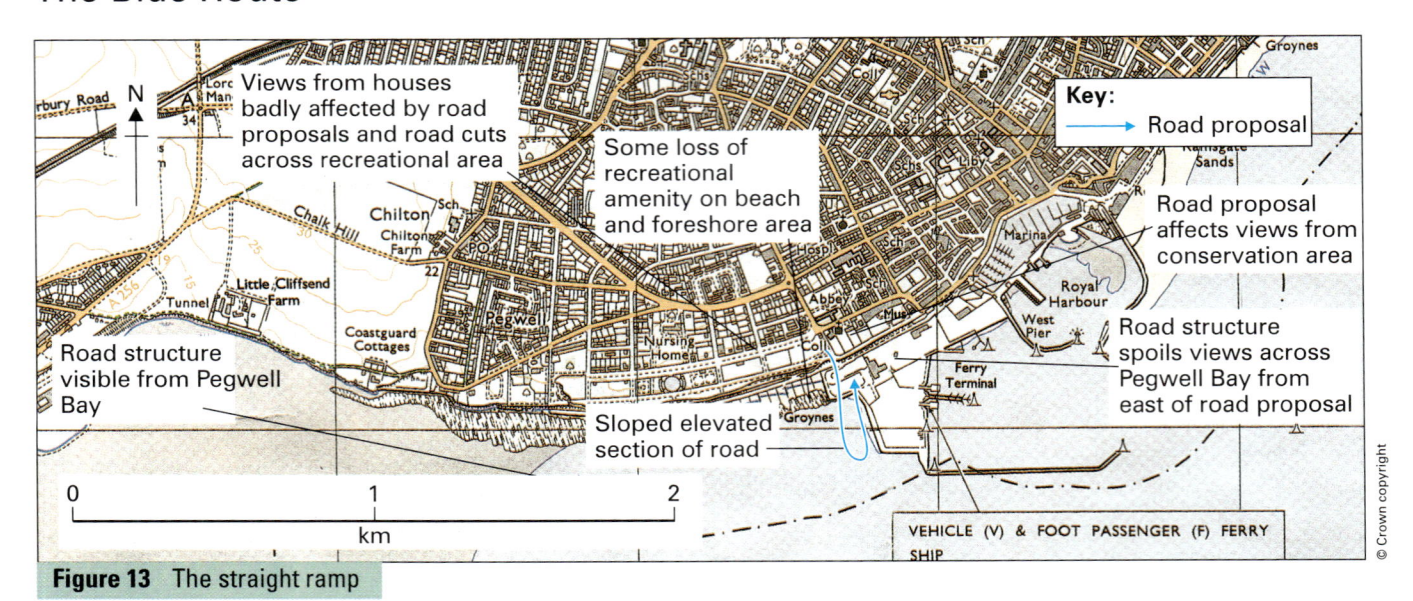

Figure 13 The straight ramp

- During construction there would be considerable disruption to part of the port area as the lower part of the ramp would be built on the existing port area.
- Pedestrian movement along the Promenade would be disrupted.
- As the new road would be within the existing harbour area, it would not affect the area of protected foreshore.
- The straight ramp would extend further seawards than the spiral ramp of the Green Route and this would have a greater impact on a wider landscape. From most viewpoints, however, it will be seen against a background of the port, thus reducing its visual impact.

- Two hectares of existing port area will be needed for the new road.
- Within the urban area some older buildings, such as The Grange, could be affected by traffic.
- The effects on air pollution, traffic noise and vibration will be the same as those for the Green Route.
- As with the Green Route, the elevated section may need to be closed during periods of severe weather, particularly to high-sided vehicles.

Improving the approach road to Ramsgate Harbour

The Decision

FOUNDATION

1. a) Study carefully all the information given about the three possible routes for the new road. Decide what the good and bad points are for each route. Construct a matrix, like the one below, for your answers. Try to think of two or three points for each box.

Route name	Good points	Bad points
Red		

   b) State one advantage that the Blue Route has over the Red Route.
2. After studying all the evidence provided:
   a) Which do you consider to be the best route?
   b) Give three reasons why you have chosen this route.
   c) For one other route, give one reason why you do not consider it to be the best choice.

HIGHER

1. Study all the information given about the three possible routes for the new road. Explain the advantages and disadvantages of each route.
2. a) Which part of the existing route to the harbour is most affected by the rapid growth of port traffic?
   b) Explain why your chosen part is so badly affected.
   c) People living in the part of Ramsgate likely to be affected by the new road have very differing views on the proposals. Explain how and why their views might differ.
3. One of the routes needs to be chosen. Decide which route you favour, giving reasons for your choice. Explain fully why you rejected the other two routes.

Summary

Ramsgate as a cross-Channel port has seen enormous growth since the 1970s. Drivers approaching the harbour area have to negotiate roads which were not designed to take the present volume and size of vehicles. People living along these roads are being subjected to increased hazards as a result – noise and air pollution, vibration and increased risk of accidents. In addition, historic buildings are under threat.

Clearly this is a situation which cannot continue; a new approach road is essential if the port is to continue to grow. Although initially there were many suggestions for such a road, these were eventually narrowed down to just three options, each of which was estimated to cost much the same. Which route would be the best for all concerned?

9 The development of Whitehills, Northampton

Background information

The Northamptonshire Structure Plan states that provision must be made for about 62 400 new dwellings in the period 1988 to 2006. Of these, 8500 should be in the Daventry District and 1000 dwellings are specifically identified as being related to the growth of Northampton.

The need for 1000 more homes in Northampton is linked to its continued development as a service and employment centre. This is likely to result in inward migration to the area. A substantial proportion of the people who will eventually live in these new houses are likely to work in the town of Northampton.

The two main options available are either the development of a site or sites on the edge of the existing town of Northampton or a dispersal of houses to a large number of smaller sites in the surrounding villages.

The major site on the edge of the existing urban area is to the north of Northampton adjacent to the Whitehills area of the town, while the villages would include places like Harlestone, Church Brampton, Chapel Brampton and Pitsford, all of which are shown on the map (Fig. 3).

Figure 1 Location of Northampton

Factors to be considered

- the effect on existing settlements – increased urban sprawl/spoilation of villages
- the effect on local roads in terms of increased traffic, accidents, etc
- the impact on the environment
- the loss of agricultural land
- the loss of open countryside and the effects on wildlife
- increased pressure on community services.

Figure 2 Which is greater – the need for new homes or the cost to the environment?

The development of Whitehills, Northampton

Figure 3 Ordnance Survey map of Northampton

89

Decision Making Exercises

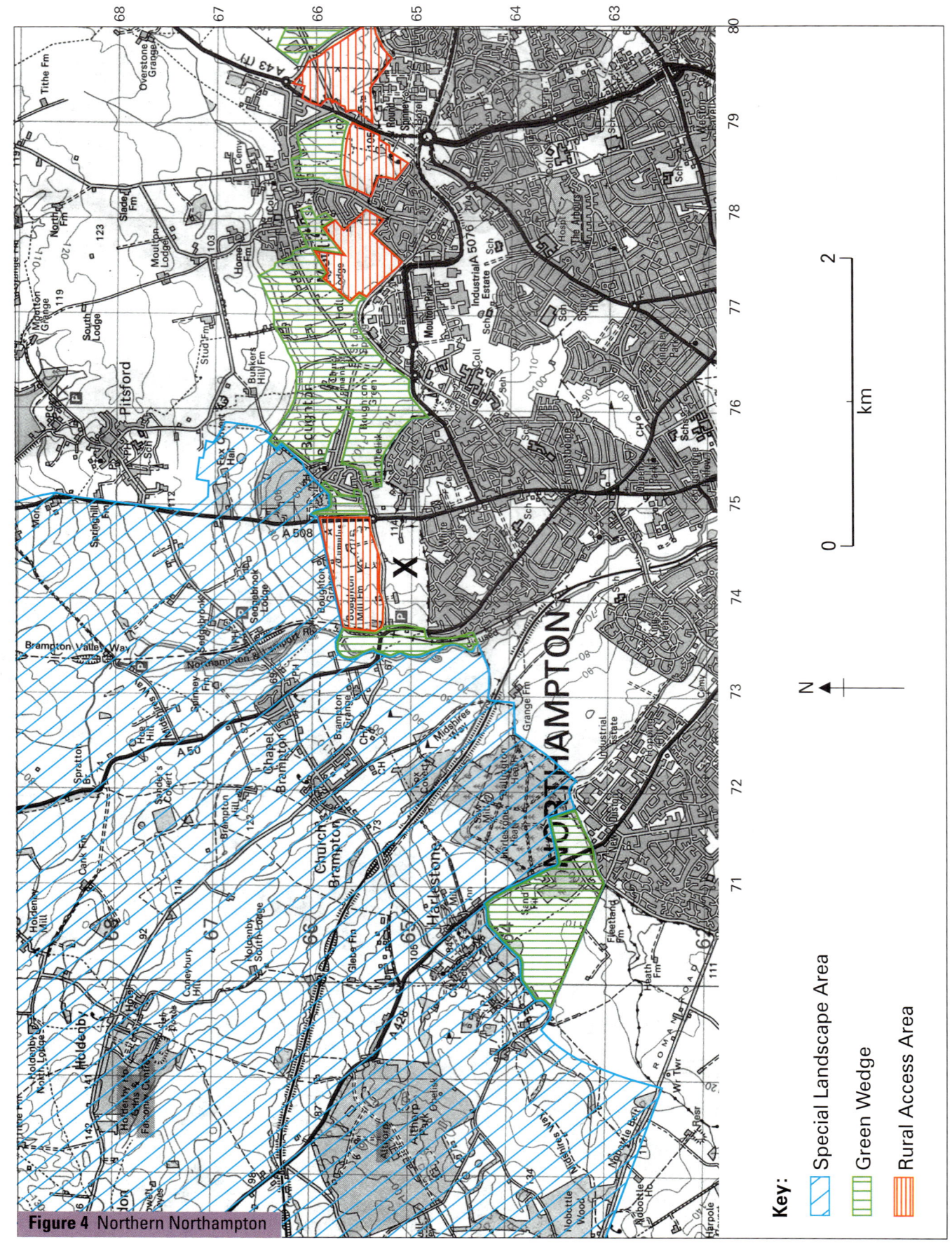

Figure 4 Northern Northampton

Key:
- Special Landscape Area
- Green Wedge
- Rural Access Area

© Crown copyright

90

The development of Whitehills, Northampton

◀ FOUNDATION ▶

1. Look at the map of the northern part of Northampton (Fig. 4).
   a) How far is the site of the proposed development (marked X on the map) from Boughton Church? (G.R. 754659)
   b) How far is it from Kingsthorpe (marked Y on the map)? (G.R. 752634)
   c) What is meant by the term 'special landscape area'?
   d) Why is only part of the rural area shown on the map referred to as a 'special landscape area'?
   e) What evidence is there on the map that local employment is available for those buying houses in the Whitehills development? Give grid references in support of your evidence.
2. Imagine you are the landlord of the public house in Chapel Brampton (G.R. 732662). Suggest reasons why you might be in favour of the new housing at Whitehills.

◀ HIGHER ▶

1. Study the map of the northern part of Northampton (Fig. 4).
   a) How far is the site for the proposed development (marked X on the map) from the church in Church Brampton? (G.R. 738657)
   b) In which compass direction is Boughton Church (G.R.754659) from the development site?
   c) What is meant by the term 'special landscape area'?
   d) What effect is this likely to have on any development proposals within that area?
   e) Give two pieces of evidence from the map which show that 'primary employment' is available in this part of Northampton. Give grid references in support of your evidence.
   f) What evidence is there that 'tertiary employment' is also available?
2. Suggest reasons why the owner of the Post Office in Chapel Brampton may be in favour of the Whitehills housing development.

BIG EXPANSION FOR NORTHAMPTON – 1000 NEW HOMES AT WHITEHILLS

ANOTHER BLOW FOR FARMING AS URBAN SPRAWL CONTINUES

VILLAGERS SAY 'NO' TO NEW HOUSING

TRADITIONAL VILLAGE UNDER THREAT

THE ONLY WAY TO SAVE THE VILLAGE SHOP IS TO EXPAND THE VILLAGE

NEW ESTATE COULD BRING CHAOS TO LOCAL SCHOOLS – OVERCROWDING IS CERTAIN

Figure 5 View south across Whitehills site

Letters to the Editor

From Mrs V. of Boughton
We are already virtually joined up to Northampton. Any development of the Whitehills site will mean that we shall just be a suburb of the town rather than a separate community.

From Mr W. of Boughton
Extra houses so close to the village could mean that we shall benefit from a better bus link to the centre of Northampton. At the moment we are virtually part of the town but don't get all the benefits.

From Mr S. of Church Brampton
At the moment my cottage overlooks open countryside, but if the Whitehills development goes ahead I shall see the edge of the town from my back windows. I shall no longer feel I live in the country.

From Mrs J. of Pitsford
We are told that any new houses at Whitehills will not be provided with a new Primary School. That means that some of the children will come to our village school rather than go into the schools in Northampton. As a result our nice little school will become overcrowded.

From Mr P. of Whitehills
A new housing estate at Whitehills could mean that our chances of getting a Community Centre in this part of Northampton are improved – we could all benefit from that.

From Miss C. (aged 9)
I could do with the opportunity for more friends. Some new houses across the road at Whitehills sounds quite exciting.

From Mrs L. of Church Brampton
A few extra customers from the new houses at Whitehills could help our village shop to survive. It is already under threat from the supermarkets in town and the out-of-town stores. Once the shop goes the village starts to die as a real living community.

From Mr T. of Boughton
Our narrow roads are already dangerous with traffic coming out of Northampton. These extra houses will just make the situation worse.

From Mr S. of Harlestone
Why keep on allowing these towns to sprawl outwards. Why not just add a few houses to each of the villages. This would help to keep the villages alive, keeping open the few remaining shops and pubs that still exist.

From Mrs M. of Whitehills
At the moment I live on the edge of the town and can walk my dog over fields. If the new houses are built at Whitehills, I shall only be able to walk him around the roads.

The development of Whitehills, Northampton

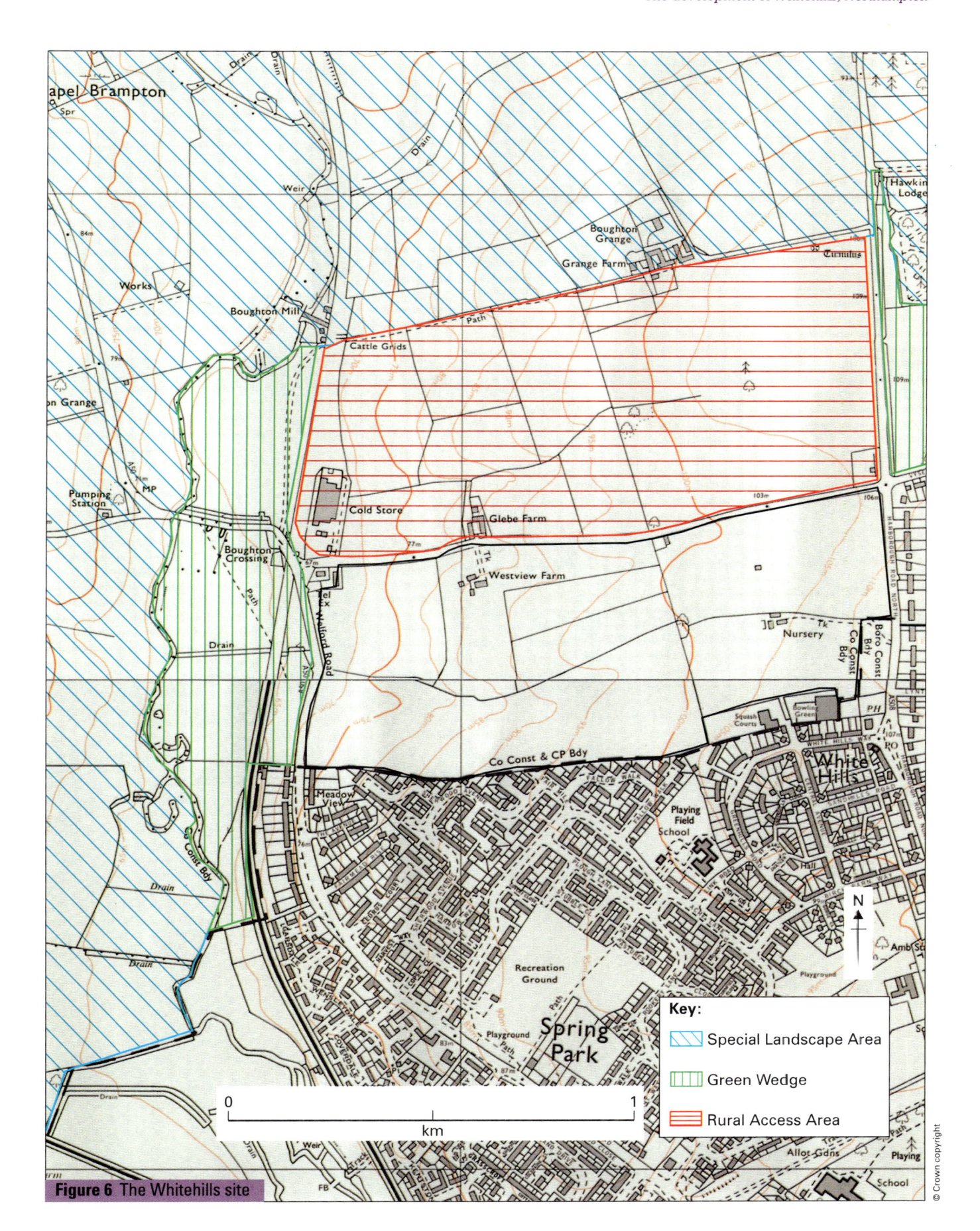

Figure 6 The Whitehills site

Key:
- Special Landscape Area
- Green Wedge
- Rural Access Area

93

The Whitehills site

Advantages

- The development would be a logical extension of the existing urban area, the adjacent farmland already being affected by closeness to the urban area (Fig. 7).
- The area is already partly built up between Boughton village and the edge of the existing urban area.
- Although agricultural land will be lost, only 3 hectares is Grade 2 land, the remainder is Grade 3.
- There is no invasion of the rural area which is designated as 'special landscape'.
- No destruction of woodland is involved, therefore only a limited loss of habitats will result.
- Pressure on local roads would be restricted due to the creation of a 'park and ride' facility and an improved bus service.
- Any improved bus service would have a 'knock-on' benefit to the residents of Boughton and Kingsthorpe.
- Shopkeepers in Boughton and Kingsthorpe would benefit from an increased number of customers.

Disadvantages

- Good agricultural land will be lost, 80 per cent being Grade 2 or Grade 3.
- It will mean that the village of Boughton will cease to be a separate community and simply become part of the urban area of Northampton.
- The edge of the existing urban area will lose its rural aspect. The houses will no longer look across open countryside.
- Local wildlife will lose valuable habitats.
- Extra traffic congestion will result on roads leading through Kingsthorpe (Fig. 8) into the town centre of Northampton.
- Local schools will become overcrowded.
- Boughton shops and pubs will become overcrowded as a result of the new housing.

Figure 7 Open countryside at the edge of the urban area

The development of Whitehills, Northampton

Extra housing in the villages

Advantages

- Extra housing will help to halt any decline in rural population.
- Village shops will benefit from extra custom which will help to keep them open.
- Small village schools will become more viable so preventing closure.
- Larger village populations could lead to the opportunity of providing a greater range of facilities.
- New housing could attract young families so encouraging a more 'normal' age structure of the population.

Disadvantages

- Extra housing could spoil the attractive appearance of the villages (Fig. 9).
- Extra traffic will be generated which could lead to narrow country roads becoming dangerous.
- Traditional village schools could be swamped by 'urban children' with different standards and attitudes.
- Urban 'migrants' would probably not use the village shop but would continue to be attracted by the town facilities.
- Newcomers would not mix in with the village community having an urban background and attitude.

Figure 8 Traffic in Kingsthorpe

Decision Making Exercises

Figure 9 Chapel Brampton village

The options

Option 1
Develop the land at Whitehills for housing, initially for 500 but eventually expanding to 1000 dwellings.

Option 2
Place the same number of houses in the surrounding rural area, a relatively small number in each village.

FOUNDATION

3 Imagine you are the Chair of Pitsford Parish Council leading a campaign against a proposed expansion of the village. Explain the main points you would put forward in your campaign.

4 Look at the map of the Whitehills development site (Fig. 6). Find Glebe Farm and Westview Farm.
The owners of these two farms have opposing views on the proposed housing development.
a) Suggest what views might be held by the two farmers.
b) Explain why their views are different.

HIGHER

3 There is a proposal to expand the village of Harlestone in order to provide more housing. Explain why the residents are divided in their views about such a proposal.

4 The owners of Glebe Farm and Westview Farm, shown on Figure 6, have opposing views about the proposed Whitehills development. Explain why they should have such different ideas when they live so close to each other.

The Decision

FOUNDATION

Look at the two options available for providing the new houses needed.
1. Choose which option you prefer and give reasons for your choice.
2. Give three reasons why you did not choose the alternative.

HIGHER

You have to decide between the two options for providing more houses in the Northampton area.
1. Choose which option you prefer and give reasons for your choice.
2. Explain why you rejected the alternative option.

Summary

Northamptonshire, like most other counties in England, is having to tackle the question of extra housing provision, not so much the question of whether or not the houses are needed, but rather where to put them. The growth of urban areas is not a new phenomenon although it is only in recent years that people have begun to realise just how much of the rural landscape is being lost under urban sprawl. In the Northampton area, for example, should the 1000 houses needed be located on one large estate on the northern edge of the town, so allowing Northampton to sprawl that little bit further, or should they be dispersed in small numbers among a range of neighbouring villages?

10 Salisbury bypass

Background information

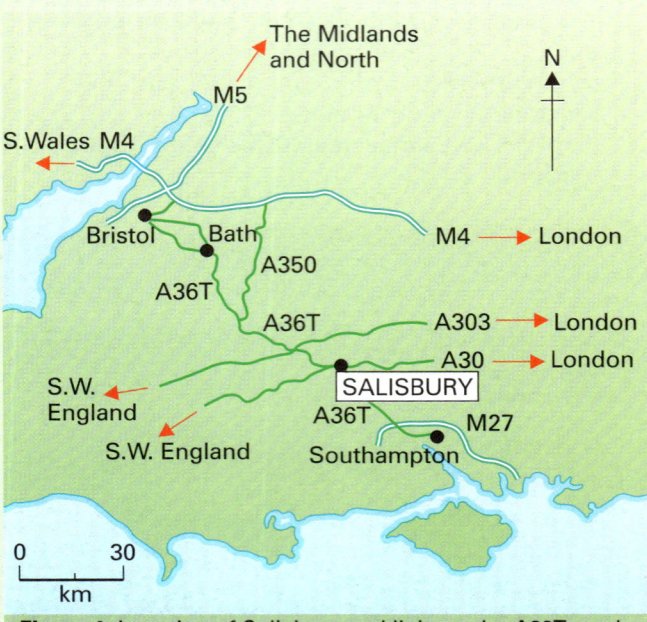

Figure 1 Location of Salisbury and links to the A36T road

The A36T road runs from the M27 west of Southampton to Bath where it connects with the A4 to Bristol, and with the A46 link to the M4 to South Wales and the M5 to the Midlands and the North. To the north-west of Salisbury the A36T links up with the A303 to Exeter and the far south-west (Fig. 1).

Therefore, the A36T (Fig. 2) can be seen as an important cross-country route directly serving several major conurbations and carrying a high proportion of heavy goods traffic. For long stretches the road is poorly aligned, sub-standard single carriageway unable to cope with the volume of traffic using it.

Since the 1970s the Department of Transport has been gradually improving the A36T although retaining mainly single carriageway. However, because of the volume of existing traffic and projected increases (Fig. 4), all new road improvements must involve dual carriageway construction.

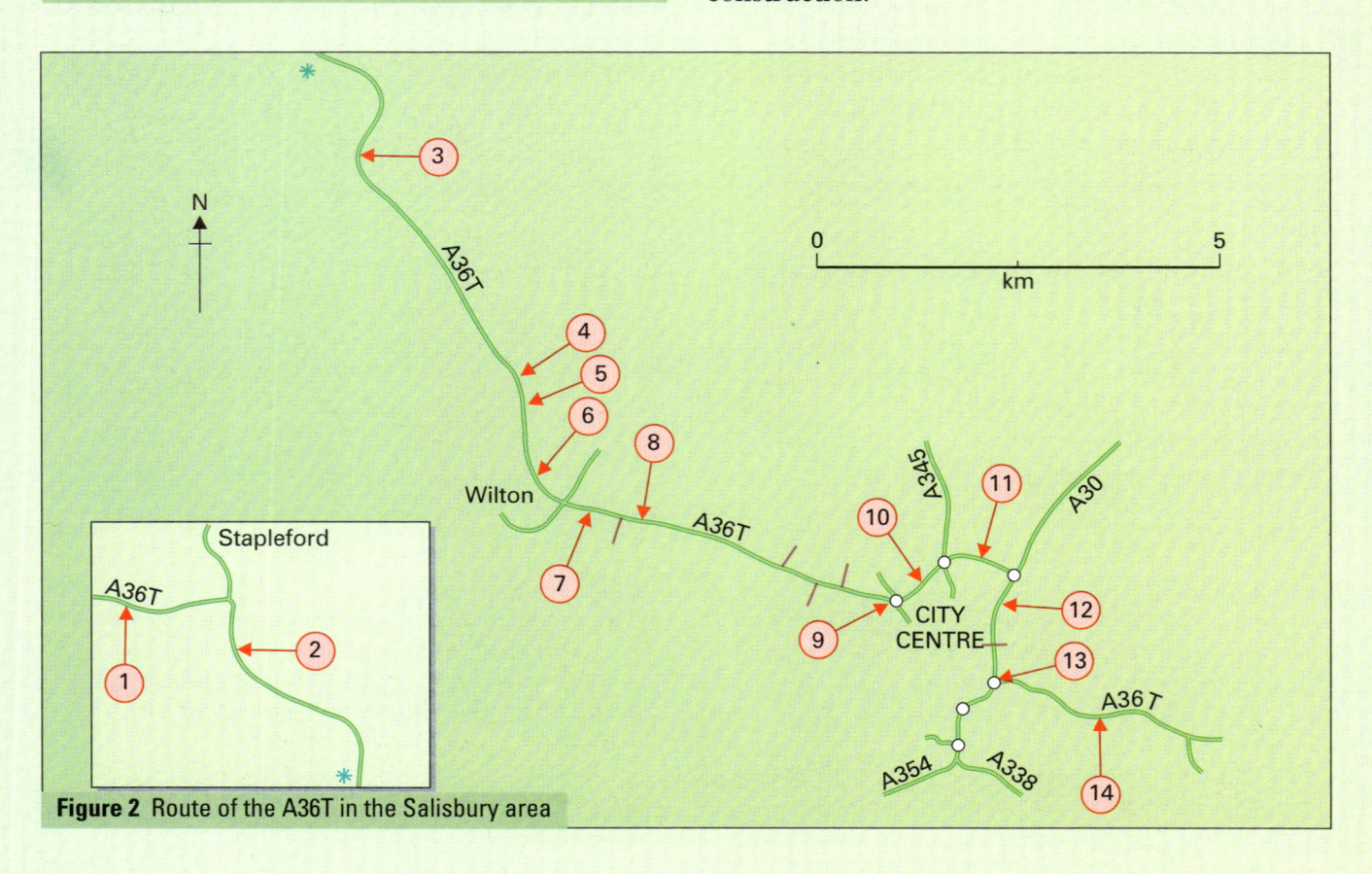

Figure 2 Route of the A36T in the Salisbury area

98

Salisbury bypass

Figure 3 Aerial view of Salisbury

The most common solution for relieving traffic congestion in towns, particularly where there is a lot of traffic, is to construct a bypass. In Salisbury plans for a bypass were first drawn up in the late 1940s. Since then, controversy has surrounded the possible route of and even the need for a bypass for the city. Lengthy public enquiries have been held at which strong arguments for and against a range of route options have been advanced. The whole city has been totally split on this issue. As with any major road scheme, government finance is involved as well as the transport policy of the day. Any change of government can bring about a change in transport policy. In fact, in July 1997, following such a change of government, the Salisbury bypass proposal was dropped from the national road improvement programme.

FOUNDATION

1. Look at Figure 1.
   a) Name the two motorways that are found close to each end of the A36T road.
   b) Which road connects the A36T north-west of Salisbury to the south-west of England?
2. Give three reasons why the present A36T road is considered to be inadequate.

HIGHER

1. Study Figure 1.
   a) Which two parts of the country are linked by the A36T road?
   b) Why is Southampton likely to generate a considerable quantity of goods traffic leading on to the A36T road?
2. Explain why many people argue that Salisbury needs a bypass.

Decision Making Exercises

Section	Status	Carriageway width (m)	Estimated notional capacity (vehicles per day)	Existing flow AADT (1990) (vehicles)	2011 without bypass Forecast flow Low	2011 without bypass Forecast flow High	2011 without bypass Degree of loading Low	2011 without bypass Degree of loading High	2011 with bypass Forecast flow Low	2011 with bypass Forecast flow High	2011 with bypass Degree of loading Low	2011 with bypass Degree of loading High
1 Serrington to junction with B3083, Stapleford	Rural single carriageway	6.0 – 7.5	8500	9300	13000	15700	Severely overloaded	Severely overloaded	<100	<100	Good	Good
2 South of B3083 to Stoford	Rural single carriageway	6.0 – 7.0	8500	10300	14400	17400	Severely overloaded	Very severely overloaded	2400	3000	Good	Good
3 South of Stoford to northern edge of South Newton	Rural single carriageway	6.0	8500	9900	13600	17600	Severely overloaded	Very severely overloaded	2700	4200	Good	Good
4 Through South Newton	Urban single carriageway Type C	6.0 – 7.0	9000	11400	15800	20200	Severely overloaded	Very severely overloaded	4900	6600	Good	Good
5 Southern limit of South Newton to railway bridge near Kingsway	Rural single carriageway	7.0	11500	11400	15800	20200	Overloaded	Severely overloaded	4900	6600	Good	Good
6 Kingsway to A30 roundabout	Urban single carriageway Type C	6.0 – 7.0	7000	12900	17000	21700	Very severely overloaded	Very severely overloaded	6700	8700	Acceptable	Just acceptable
7 East of A30 Roundabout to Netherhampton Road	Rural single carriageway	8.0 – 10.0	14500	25300	36000	41900	Very severely overloaded	Very severely overloaded	23400	26000	Severely overloaded	Severely overloaded
8 East of Netherhampton Road to West of Skew Bridge	Rural single carriageway	8.0	14500	18400	23100	26400	Severely overloaded	Severely overloaded	20200	21900	Overloaded	Severely overloaded
9 Skew Bridge to West of St Paul's Roundabout	Urban single carriageway Type C	8.0 – 10.0	16000	25000	31800	35400	Severely overloaded	Very severely overloaded	22600	28100	Overloaded	Severely overloaded
10 St Paul's Roundabout to Castle St Roundabout	Urban dual carriageway Type B	14.6	44500	34300	44700	53800	Acceptable	Just acceptable	29100	33900	Good	Good
11 East of Castle St Roundabout to St Mark's Roundabout	Urban dual carriageway Type B	14.6	44500	34900	48000	54900	Acceptable	Just acceptable	27700	30200	Good	Good
12 South of St Mark's Roundabout to College Roundabout	Urban dual carriageway Type B	14.6	44500	35700	56500	66100	Just acceptable	Overloaded	33600	37200	Good	Good
13 East of College Roundabout to Tesco's Roundabout	Urban wide single carriageway Type B	9.0	18000	29900	45800	52300	Very severely overloaded	Very severely overloaded	25900	29000	Overloaded	Severely overloaded
14 East of Tesco's Roundabout to Alderbury Bypass	Rural single carriageway	6.0 – 8.0	11500	22800	32300	36900	Very severely overloaded	Very severely overloaded	7500	8800	Good	Acceptable

Figure 4 Existing and projected capacity of the A36T

© Crown copyright

BYPASS WILL BRING RELIEF TO TOWNS AND VILLAGES

... *significant volumes of through traffic will be removed from towns and villages along the existing A36T as well as from the central area of Salisbury.*

CUTTINGS TO DESTROY THE CHALK LANDSCAPE

... the present unspoilt rolling chalk landscape will be gouged by 12 m to 18 m deep cuttings as part of the new bypass.

FOUNDATION

3 Look at the map of the A36T road in the Salisbury area (Fig. 2) and the chart which gives information about the road and its capacity (Fig. 4).
   a) Which stretch of the present road is the narrowest?
   b) Which stretch is widest?
   c) What is meant by the term 'notional capacity'?
   d) Which stretch of the A36T had the greatest overload in 1990?
   e) Suggest why the stretches of road numbered 10, 11 and 12 on the map should have traffic figures in 1990 well below the notional capacity.

4 Look at the chart (Fig. 4).
   a) What does the chart suggest about likely road conditions which would result from a bypass not being built?
   b) What difference would a bypass make? Give evidence from the chart to support your answer.

5 Look at the chart (Fig. 4).
   a) Which part of the existing A36T would be chiefly affected by continuing overload even if a bypass is built?
   b) Suggest two reasons why, even if a bypass was to be built, there would still be traffic problems in Salisbury.

HIGHER

3 Study the map of the A36T road in the Salisbury area (Fig. 2) and the chart which gives information about the road and its capacity (Fig. 4).
   a) What is the width variation of the road?
   b) Using evidence from the Ordnance Survey map of Salisbury (Fig. 8), suggest reasons why sections 13 and 14 of the road should have experienced some of the worst overload in 1990.
   c) Give reasons why the stretches of road numbered 10, 11 and 12 should have had traffic well below the notional capacity.

4 Study the chart (Fig. 4).
   a) Using evidence from the chart, explain what is likely to happen to the A36T road without a bypass.
   b) How does the chart provide evidence that Salisbury needs a bypass?
   c) Which parts of the A36T road would benefit most from a bypass?

5 'The bypass will not solve all the traffic problems of Salisbury.' Do you agree with this statement? Use evidence from the chart (Fig. 4) to support your view.

Decision Making Exercises

The present road

- **Traffic flows** – Parts of the road carry between 50 per cent and 100 per cent more than the Department of Transport notional capacity. Other sections of the road also have traffic flows that exceed notional capacity at peak times.

- **Accidents** – Parts of the existing road have accident rates well above the national average, with up to twice the national average in parts.

- **Road conditions** – The road often suffers from poor visibility. Some low bridges mean that large vehicles have to occupy the centre of the road in order to negotiate the bridge. Junctions and side turnings are frequent so that the free flow of traffic is often interrupted.

CONSTABLE'S LANDSCAPE TO BE LOST FOREVER

... the view of meadow, spire and sky captured by John Constable's painting, and little changed since, will disappear once the bypass is built ... replaced by a necklace of concrete over 18 km long and knotted with 6 huge junctions.

BYPASS WILL NOT SORT OUT LOCAL TRAFFIC PROBLEMS

Figure 5 Traffic at Castle Street roundabout

Figure 6 Traffic in South Newton, looking north-west

NEW ROAD THREATENS RARE MEADOW AND OTHER SSSIs

... the River Avon and its tributaries are probably the best surviving chalk stream system in Britain and probably the most important in the world.

BYPASS TO GIVE FINE VIEWS

... drivers on the new bypass will enjoy fine views of the open countryside and of the cathedral.

TRAFFIC INCREASE IN SALISBURY, BYPASS OR NO BYPASS

... the city itself will remain congested and the situation will get worse.

Decision Making Exercises

Figure 7 Traffic west of Skew Bridge

BYPASS TO CUT CITY CENTRE CONGESTION

... through traffic will be removed from the inner relief road so allowing room for the diversion of more local traffic from the city centre.

LITTLE RELIEF FOR CHURCHILL WAY

... even with the bypass there will still be some problems at peak periods on the existing inner relief road, particularly at junctions.

Figure 8 Three proposed routes for the bypass

Decision Making Exercises

Assessing the three routes for the bypass

1 Option 1 – The Red Route

- **Landscape impact** – Three of the five rivers which make up the Avon system would have massive earth embankments across their floodplains: the Avon itself, the Nadder, and the Wylye which is crossed twice. There would be deep cuttings (up to 18 m deep) through the chalk, and the unspoilt view of the cathedral from open countryside would be ruined. This route would cause visual obstruction for 44 properties and visual intrusion for 139 properties.

- **Ecology** – Most of the route across the Avon meadows is within a conservation area and the route would violate the proposed SSSI for the Avon Valley in at least four places. The Avon Valley is also expected to be designated a European Special Area for Conservation. The East Harnham Meadows contain 14 hectares (ha) of a grassland type so rare that only 200 ha remain in the whole of Britain.

- **Noise** – 538 properties are within 300 m of the route.

- **Traffic relief** – Most of the through traffic on the A36T should have been removed from Churchill Way, the inner relief road, but this route would achieve only a minimal reduction in volume of traffic on the north side of the city and in the city centre where the majority of traffic is fairly local in character.

2 Option 2 – The Blue Route

- **Landscape impact** – This route would have a substantial adverse impact on the Woodford Valley, crossing it on a bridge and a 10 m high embankment near the Woodford Conservation Area. It would also have a major impact on the Woodford Water Meadow SSSI. It would cause visual obstruction to 56 properties and visual intrusion for 182 properties.

- **Ecology** – Woodford Valley experiences little human disturbance and, as such, provides a superb area for a wide variety of wildlife. The valley is of great significance to nature conservation.

- **Noise** – 174 properties are within 300 m of the route.

- **Traffic relief** – This route would ease traffic on the A36T but would have little effect on the roads to the south of Salisbury, being too far north.

Option 3 – The Green Route

- **Landscape impact** – More than 11 km of the route lies within the Area of Outstanding Natural Beauty, mainly in countryside unaffected by existing major roads. The line of the road would be totally unsympathetic, striking across the grain of the landscape and with substantial loss of woodland. The crossing of the River Nadder near Ugford and Bulbridge would be intrusive, and the route would impinge into the Wilton parkland at Hare Warren. There would be visual intrusion for 105 properties (compared with 139 for the Red Route).

- **Ecology** – The Green Route would have advantages over the Red Route in that there would be only one crossing of the River Wylye, and the crossing of the River Nadder would be shorter. However, it would bisect the Ebsbury Down SSSI of extremely diverse chalk grassland which contains national restricted species and Ebsbury Copse of ancient oak woodland. The route would also cut through Grovely Wood which comprises one of the largest tracts of ancient semi-natural woodland in Wiltshire and is one of the county's more important ornithological sites.

- **Noise** – 46 properties are within 300 m of the proposed road (compared with 538 for the Red Route) but it would create noise close to the Odstock Hospital.

- **Archaeology** – At Ebsbury Copse this route would spoil extensive Iron Age and Romano-British earthworks.

A major advantage of this route is that it avoids the Bemerton/Westwood area and it would be less expensive than the Red Route.

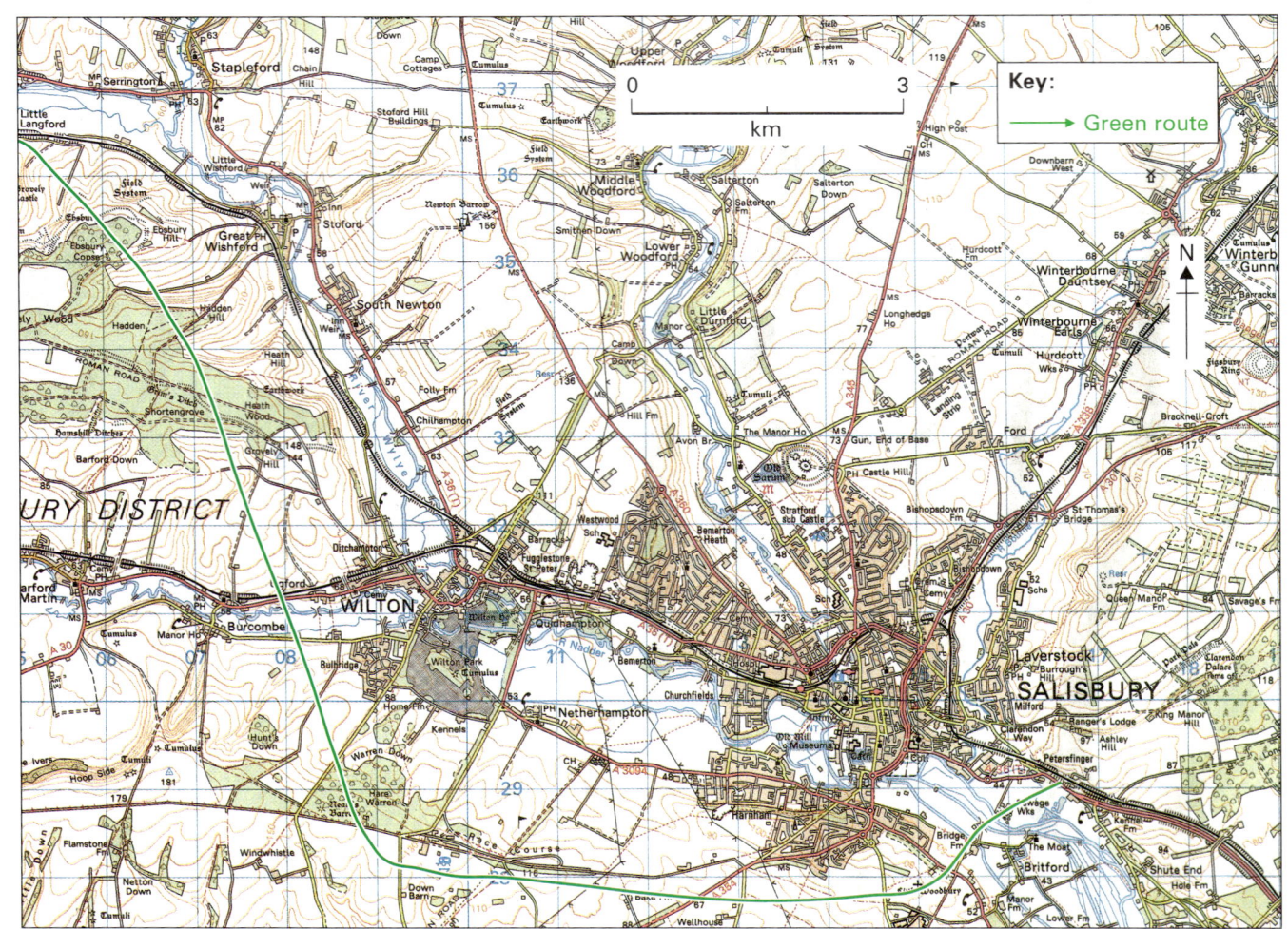

Salisbury bypass

The Decision

FOUNDATION

You have to decide between the three options for the route of the bypass. The three routes are shown on Figure 8.
1. Choose which route you prefer and give reasons for your choice.
2. Give three reasons why you did not choose either of the alternatives.
3. Do you agree with the government's decision to scrap the plans for a bypass? Give reasons to support your view.

HIGHER

You have to recommend one of the three routes for the bypass. The three possible routes are shown on Figure 8.
1. Choose which route you recommend and give your reasons.
2. Explain why you oppose the other two routes.
3. Do you agree with the government's decision to scrap the plans for a bypass? Give reasons to support your view.

Summary

Many towns are becoming choked with traffic, and Salisbury is no exception. Frequently, the suggested solution is 'build a bypass', the thought in this case being that this will return Salisbury to how it was in the early 1950s when traffic volume was only a fraction of its present figure. Experience now shows that a bypass does not necessarily solve everything. Clearly, the route of or the need for a Salisbury bypass is not easily determined. The city itself has a very favoured setting, particularly the area around the Cathedral with, as yet, many unspoilt views. The city is also surrounded by many areas of either outstanding landscape quality or scientific interest. The whole question of the bypass generates widely divergent views, and there is no easy solution. The fact that the government has decided to abandon the idea of a bypass does not mean that the problems associated with Salibury's traffic will disappear; they can only get worse! Clearly other possible solutions will need to be considered with some urgency if Salisbury is not to grind to a halt completely.

11 Saving wetlands in Doñana

Background information

Doñana is situated in Andalusia in south-west Spain (Fig. 1). It is part of the extensive low, flat area of marshes known as Las Marismas which were formed by the Guadalquivir river. It is the most important **wetland** of Spain, and also the most important of Europe. Interest in the ecological value of wetlands was not developed until the 1970s. Prior to this date wetlands had been drained to provide land for agricultural purposes and for new settlement. Since the 1960s Spain has lost 60 per cent of its wetlands. In the early 1990s 40 000 hectares (ha) of wetlands have disappeared mainly because of overexploitation of groundwater.

The fate of Doñana is a much debated issue. The area which is now Doñana National Park has been legally protected since 1969. It was declared a national park in 1978 and a World Heritage Site in 1996. It is being threatened by factors outside its boundaries in the Natural Park (Fig. 6). The Natural Park was created in 1989 and covers 54 000 ha. A more flexible approach to nature protection is permitted, and economic development is also allowed. These activities are threatening the National Park's very existence by lowering the **water table** which results in desiccation and the destruction of habitats. Overexploitation of groundwater by agriculture, tourism and residential development is now a major issue, but equally so is the provision of jobs in this region, one of the poorest in Europe.

Figure 1 Location of Doñana

Doñana National Park fact file

- 50 720 ha
- Lies between 0 m and 10 m above sea level.
- Semi-arid region; annual rainfall 565 mm, falling in the period from autumn to spring; wettest months are December and January, each 90 mm. Parts of the park dried up in the drought in the early 1990s. December and January 9.3 °C, July and August 24.4 °C.
- Three basic zones (Fig. 3):
  - Mobile sand dunes up to 30 m high lie parallel to the coast; blown inland by the prevailing south-west wind; occupy about 10 per cent of park. One of the most important dune systems in Europe (Fig. 4).
  - Stable sands.
- Wetlands (about 52 per cent): area of salt marsh, deep channels (canos) streams and lakes. In winter flooded to a depth of 0.3 m; several shallow lakes remain in summer. Cork oaks at edge of marsh important for nesting.
- Each habitat has a different ecosystem resulting in a great variety of flora and fauna.
- Particularly important for birds:
  - wintering quarters of greylag geese
  - flamingos
  - imperial eagles (endangered species)
  - herons.
- Noted animals include wild boar, lynx (endangered) deer and mongoose.

Saving wetlands in Doñana

Figure 2 Aerial view of Doñana National Park

Figure 3 Zones of Doñana National Park

Key:
— Doñana National Park boundary
↓ Wetland
— Road
▮ Sand

111

Decision Making Exercises

Figure 4 Mobile sand dunes

Figure 5 The wetlands are flooded in winter and spring

1 Using Figures 2 and 3 identify on Figure 2
   a) the National Park boundary
   b) the River Guadalquivir and Guadiamar
   c) lakes – Lucio de los Ansares and Lucio del Membritto
   d) the wetlands
   e) the mobile dunes.

2 Describe the coast and estimate its length.
3 Using Figure 5 describe the wetland scene.
4 Look at Figure 1 and give a reason why Doñana lies on a bird migration route.
5 Give as many reasons as possible why Doñana should be saved.

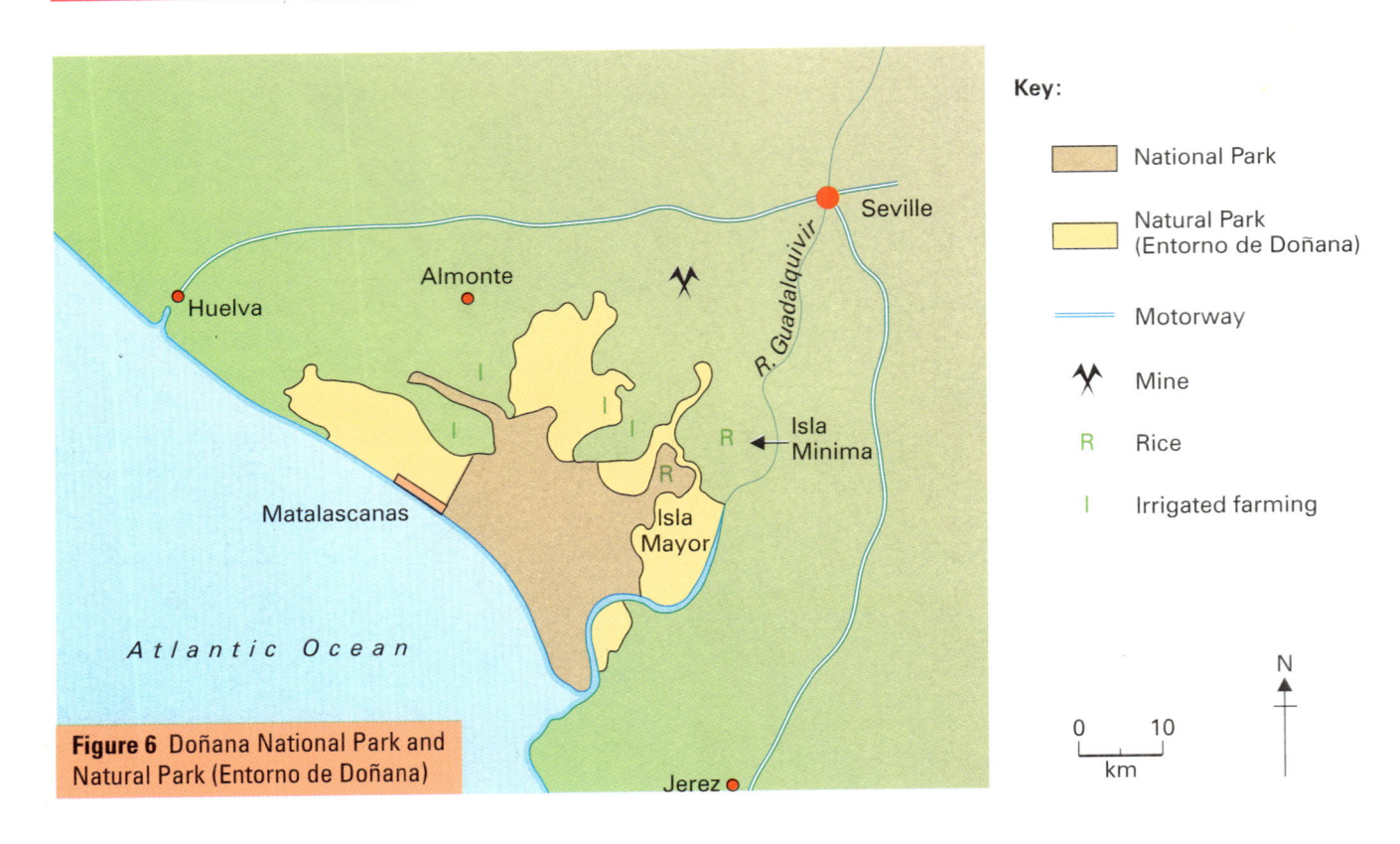

Figure 6 Doñana National Park and Natural Park (Entorno de Doñana)

Key:
- National Park
- Natural Park (Entorno de Doñana)
- Motorway
- Mine
- R Rice
- I Irrigated farming

112

The problem

Doñana is under threat from developments outside and within the National Park. The biggest threat from outside the park is overexploitation of water.

Agriculture – viewpoints

Farming has always been an activity in the area around the wetlands but there were fewer farmers and they did not use intensive methods. The aquifer was being recharged at a rate higher than that at which water was being abstracted. There was enough water for Doñana and for agriculture.

Until the 1930s the region was of little economic value. Then the government decided to introduce rice cultivation. The most important areas were in Isla Mayor and Isla Minima. Today 40 per cent of Spain's rice comes from this area.

In 1971 a new phase of farming started. A large underground supply of water was discovered in the late 1960s. This prompted the government to go ahead with a large-scale irrigation scheme: the Almonte–Marismas Irrigation Plan.

By 1986 there were 7000 ha of irrigated farmland. 50 million m^3 of water are pumped annually. The expansion was encouraged by EU farm policy. Markets in Western Europe guaranteed high prices for our new products – vegetables, fruit and flowers.

By 1992 the area under irrigation had increased to 10 000 ha – that is 3000 ha more than is advisable for the safety of the area. The water table is being drastically lowered to irrigate thirsty crops like strawberries (Fig. 7) – five crops a year are produced on the sandy soils.

Water pollution has now become a problem. Pesticides are used in rice cultivation and growing of strawberries. The polluted water finds its way underground and affects Doñana. Park boundaries do not provide boundaries against the movement of water above or below ground. Thousands of birds have been poisoned.

Figure 7 Strawberry picking

Decision Making Exercises

Tourism – viewpoints

The main centre for tourists is Matalascanas (Fig. 8) just outside the National Park. It was built in the late 1960s when mass tourism hit Spain (and destroyed many of our coastal wetlands).

There were plans to build another resort, Costa Doñana, to the west of Matalascanas but permission was refused because of the threat it posed to the water table under the dunes. It was an ambitious complex with 20 000 hotel placements (Fig. 9).

Plans for developing tourism along the Huelva coast also included the building of a large number of residential units. Inland, El Rocio at the gateway to the park also expanded. It was just a small village until the 1950s.

Tourism provides much needed jobs but we are worried because tourist numbers have fallen recently.

Matalascanas is also a major threat to our underground water supplies. Over 100 000 visitors come here each year, mainly in the summer when the aquifer is not being recharged. 1000 million litres of water are consumed each year. Water is not only used for drinking and for domestic uses but for watering hotel lawns.

Another plan to develop a tourist complex on the left bank of the Guadalquivir at Sanlucar eventually got the go-ahead in November 1996. The river will act as a natural barrier and so Doñana will not be affected by water abstraction.

Figure 8 Matalascanas

Saving wetlands in Doñana

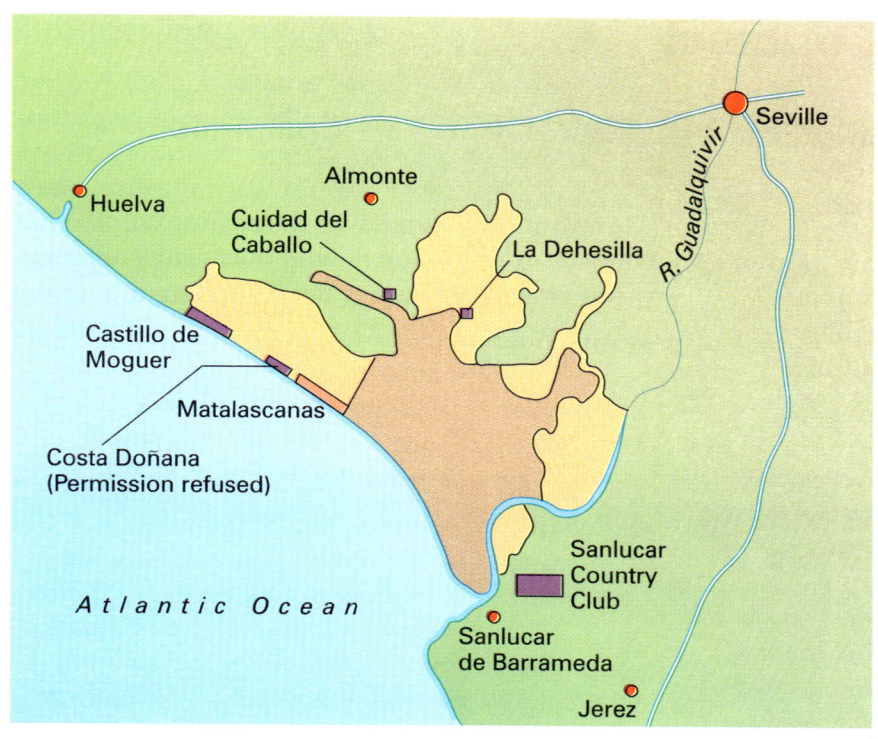

Figure 9 Tourism developments

Other threats

There are several other external threats to Doñana. These include pollution of water by industrial waste and urban effluent from cities further upstream, and pollution from the lead and copper mines to the north as poisonous slurry is washed down into the fragile wetland. Not only is the environment adversely affected by pollution but so are people; many villagers have suffered respiratory diseases and dermatitis, for example. In the 1990s new threats include further tourism projects (luxury residential units), gas pipelines, more roads such as Trazado Norte, and a barrage on the Guadalquivir.

FOUNDATION

1. In which year did large-scale irrigated farming start? How did this affect underground water supplies?
2. Why do farmers grow crops such as fruit and vegetables which need lots of water?
3. Why does tourism use vast quantities of water?
4. Why is the development of tourism important for the local people?
5. a) List three other types of development outside the National Park which are a threat to the park.
   b) For each development state one way in which it affects the park.

HIGHER

1. a) Explain why farming did not adversely affect Doñana National Park before 1971.
   b) Study Figures 2 and 3 again and identify the farmed areas.
2. Explain why farmers continue to practise a type of farming which adversely affects the environment.
3. a) What natural factors encouraged the development of tourism?
   b) Why is this activity harmful to the environment?
4. Draw a spider diagram to show the ways in which the National Park is threatened by activities outside its boundaries. Explain why this is so.
5. Why are people concerned about the projected tourism developments?

Decision Making Exercises

Assessing the three options

Option 1 – Conservation of Doñana

This would mean no development in the surrounding area which would, in turn, mean no new jobs. With an increasing population this would result in growing unemployment. Furthermore, wages are low and people are struggling to make a living.

Option 2 – Development in the surrounding area without due regard for the effects on Doñana

Plans have been put forward for further luxury residential units for tourists at Castillo de Moguer, Cuidad del Caballo and La Dehesilla. These would all make further demands on the underground water supplies of the National Park, increasing the already serious situation (Fig. 9).

Option 3 – Sustainable development

This means thinking of the future instead of short-term development with quick gains which would damage the environment.

- Green farming:
  - diversify farming, for example grow traditional crops such as olives and oranges which do not make demands on water
  - provide subsidies.
- Ecotourism
  - expand tourism in Doñana National Park – at present, visitors have only limited access – viewing platforms; four-hour guided tour by Land Rover; park could handle more visitors: 1981 40 000; 1995 250 000
  - improve park management (e.g. too many wild boar in places resulting in overgrazing)
  - develop small-scale tourism in the villages – locals would benefit by offering services, craft industries
  - extend the tourist season.
- Subsidies for water-related projects
  - to conserve natural supplies
  - to find additional sources.

Figure 10 Gathering shellfish on the beach at Doñana – a traditional occupation

The Decision

FOUNDATION

1. Divide your page into four columns headed: Option number; Advantages for the environment; Disadvantages for the environment; Economic advantages. Then complete your table by filling in the information for each of the three options.
2. Study your table carefully.
   a) Which scheme benefits both the environment and the people?
   b) Give three reasons for your decision.

HIGHER

1. Decide, giving reasons, which option you think should be adopted.
2. For one of the other options explain why you think the scheme is not advisable.

Summary

Doñana, a unique wetland, is under threat. Until the 1930s, when the government introduced rice growing, it was of little economic importance. The real threat came in the 1960s with the rapid development of agriculture and tourism in the surrounding area, both making enormous demands on underground water supplies. The result of this was the dramatic lowering of the water table, thereby destroying habitats in the park. In the 1990s, further projects threaten the park. The region is one of the least developed parts of Spain and one of the poorest in Europe. What is the way forward?

Glossary

sustainable development development without damage to the environment

water table upper level of water stored underground in permeable rocks

wetlands shallow water environments, either temporarily or permanently flooded

12 Flood alleviation in the Lavant Valley, Chichester

Background information

The River Lavant is a short stream, only 13 km long, which rises north-east of Chichester (West Sussex) and discharges into the sea at the northern end of Fishbourne Channel. For most of its course the Lavant is unembanked but it is contained in artificial channels and **culverts** through Chichester. It has a small topographic **catchment**: only 95 km^2 (Fig. 4). The upper part of the catchment lies on the chalk dip slope of the South Downs. Downstream of Westhampnett Mill is the lower catchment lying on the gravels of the coastal plain. The main **aquifer** is the chalk, which is **permeable**. Most of the rain falling on this rock quickly finds its way underground, and it is this groundwater which is mainly responsible for the flow of the Lavant, a typical seasonal chalk stream. It is not unusual for the stream to be dry especially in summer, but at the end of October, fed by chalk springs, it begins to flow again (Figs. 2 and 3).

Figure 1 Location of Chichester

Figure 2 River Lavant at Singleton, close to its present source. In 1994 the village was flooded. In April 1997, following almost two years of low rainfall, the driest period for 150 years, the stream had little water reflecting the low level of underground water resources.

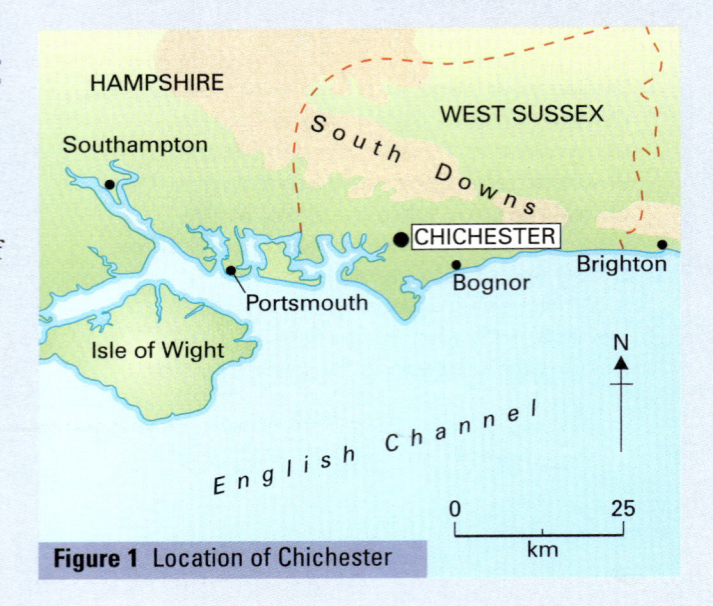

Figure 3 River Lavant at East Lavant, spring 1997. A placid stream, the water is approximately 10 cm deep following a period of drought.

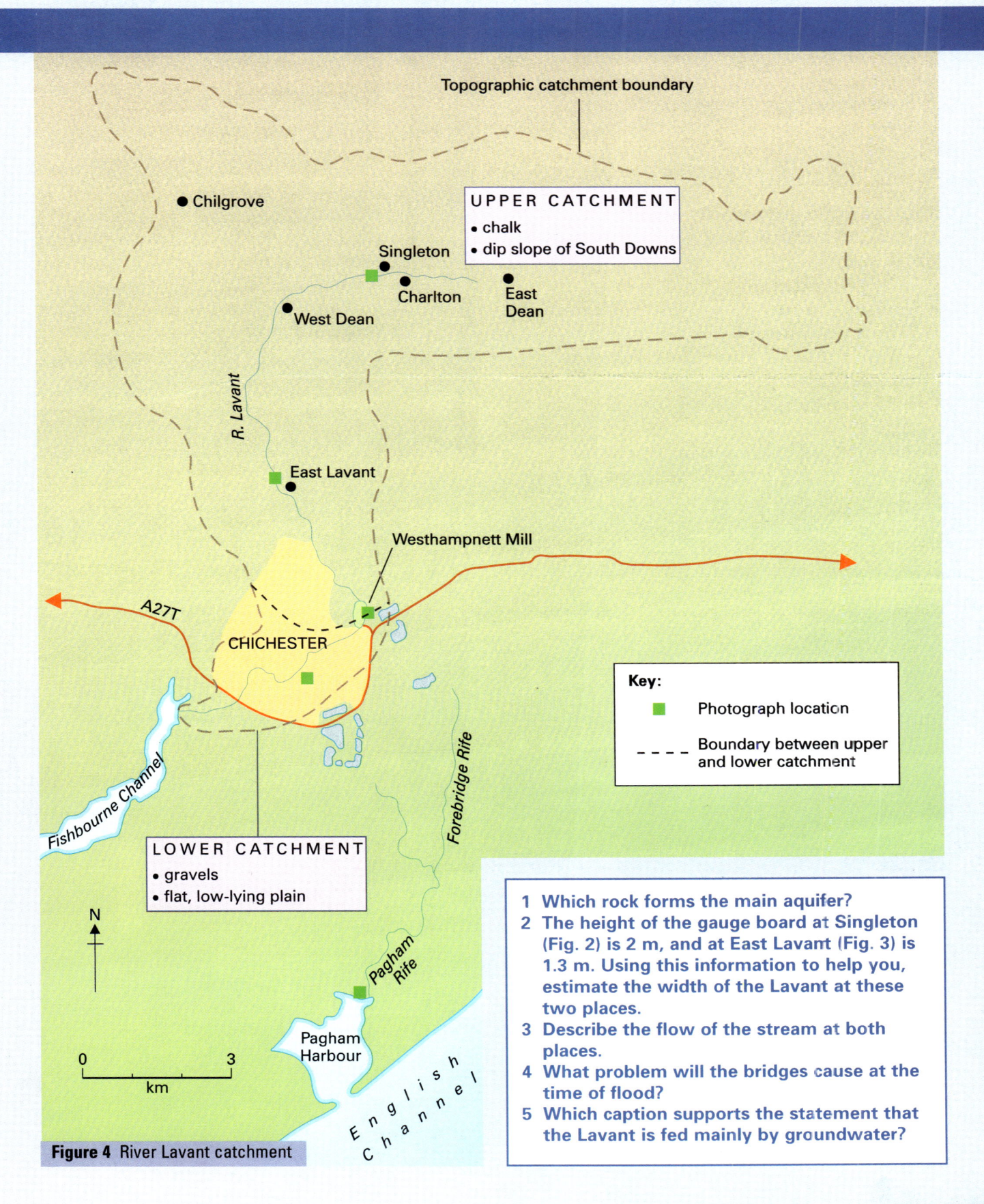

Flood alleviation in the Lavant Valley, Chichester

Figure 4 River Lavant catchment

Topographic catchment boundary

• Chilgrove

UPPER CATCHMENT
• chalk
• dip slope of South Downs

Singleton
Charlton
West Dean
East Dean

R. Lavant

East Lavant

Westhampnett Mill

A27T

CHICHESTER

Fishbourne Channel

Forebridge Rife

LOWER CATCHMENT
• gravels
• flat, low-lying plain

Pagham Harbour

Pagham Rife

English Channel

Key:
■ Photograph location
- - - - Boundary between upper and lower catchment

0 ——— 3
km

1 Which rock forms the main aquifer?
2 The height of the gauge board at Singleton (Fig. 2) is 2 m, and at East Lavant (Fig. 3) is 1.3 m. Using this information to help you, estimate the width of the Lavant at these two places.
3 Describe the flow of the stream at both places.
4 What problem will the bridges cause at the time of flood?
5 Which caption supports the statement that the Lavant is fed mainly by groundwater?

Decision Making Exercises

History of flooding

The River Lavant has a long history of flooding (Fig. 5). In the twentieth century flooding in Chichester was recorded in 1927 and again in 1960 when extensive areas of the city were affected.

The 1994 flood event

The serious flooding which occurred in early January 1994 was the worst in living memory. It was caused by:
- above average rainfall (Fig. 9, p.123)
- culverts and natural channels unable to cope with the volume of water
  • natural channel above Chichester: 5.5 **cumecs** capacity
  • culverts under Chichester: 4.5 cumecs capacity.

Records indicate that when the **discharge** of floodwater moving down the valley below Westhampnett Mill is greater than 4.2 cumecs, the culverts and bridges restrict the flow and flooding results, not only in parts of the city centre but also at Westhampnett Mill (Fig. 6).

Date	History of flooding
1713	St Pancras and the Hornet areas
1763	St Pancras and the Hornet areas
1771	The Hornet area
1804	Cellars in various locations
1809	St Pancras and the Hornet areas
1826	Cellars of more than half the houses in the city filled; further more serious flooding a week later in St Pancras area
1839	The Hornet area: flooding caused by almost continuous rains of preceding year
1852	St Pancras and the Hornet areas after almost six weeks of continuous rain

Figure 5 Record of flooding in Chichester in the eighteenth and nineteenth centuries

Figure 6 Westhampnett Mill, scene of widespread flooding in 1994, was dry in early April 1997

Flood alleviation in the Lavant Valley, Chichester

Look at the newspaper clips and Figure 8 to see how Chichester was affected by the 1994 flooding.

CHICHESTER DAILY
1 January 1994

Intense storm brings heavy rainfall: 50 mm falls in 4 hours

CHICHESTER DAILY
5 January 1994

AMBER ALERT FOR R. LAVANT

The Lavant valley is awash after weeks of rain and has been placed on amber alert (flooding likely). Shops in the Hornet area of Chichester have been flooded to a depth of several feet. The West Sussex Fire Brigade has started a massive pumping operation.

West Sussex Gazette
11 January 1994

CHICHESTER CUT OFF

As snow thaw added to the already high river levels, all major roads from the east into Chichester were virtually impassable. The flow of the Lavant is now four times its average. The army has been called in to build bailey bridges across the flooded A27 and A259. Extra staff and a sand-bagging machine have been brought in from the *NRA's Anglian region to help sandbag the sides of the A259 Chichester–Bognor Regis road in an attempt to keep it open [Fig. 8].

Chichester Evening News
7 January 1994

LAVANT ON RED ALERT
EMERGENCY CONTROL ROOM IN COUNTY HALL

CHICHESTER DAILY
6 January 1994

A27 flooded at Westhampnett Mill
16 Green Goddesses brought in from the North

Pumping got underway yesterday to relieve flooding in the Hornet area of town. The floodwater is being pumped through the city and out to sea, a distance of three miles or so.

CHICHESTER DAILY
1 February 1994

PUMPING OPERATIONS SCALED DOWN

The Lavant was downgraded to amber alert yesterday. Although groundwater levels have dropped seven metres in the last ten days, they are still high. A *NRA spokesperson says that the risk of flooding remains. Consultants have now been called in to investigate the cause of flooding, the worst for 130 years.

* NRA: National Rivers Authority which from 1 April 1996 became the Environment Agency.

Figure 7 1994 floods in the Hornet area

121

Decision Making Exercises

Key:
- ← - - - Emergency 15 cm pipes
- B Bailey bridge
- H Hornet
- St P St Pancras
- Floodwater

Figure 8 Extent of January 1994 floods

Flood alleviation in the Lavant Valley, Chichester

Above average rainfall
- heavy rainfall Sept–Oct
- more rain in late Dec
- unusually heavy rainfall early Jan
- Sept 1993–Jan 1994 rainfall: 750 mm, 40% of which fell 6 Dec–14 Jan
- South Downs av. rainfall Sept–Jan: 490 mm

→

Very high groundwater levels
- Chilgrove well:

date	depth of water
1.12.93	50 m
10.1.94	77.18 m
20.1.94	level began to fall

→ **Springs broke out all round catchment**

↓

River flow increased
- end Oct: 0.1 cumecs
- end Dec: 1.7 cumecs
- 13 Jan: 7.9 cumecs
- 31 Jan: 5.5 cumecs

FLOODING 4 JAN–22 JAN

↑

Water from higher ground ran off into river (surface run-off)

↑

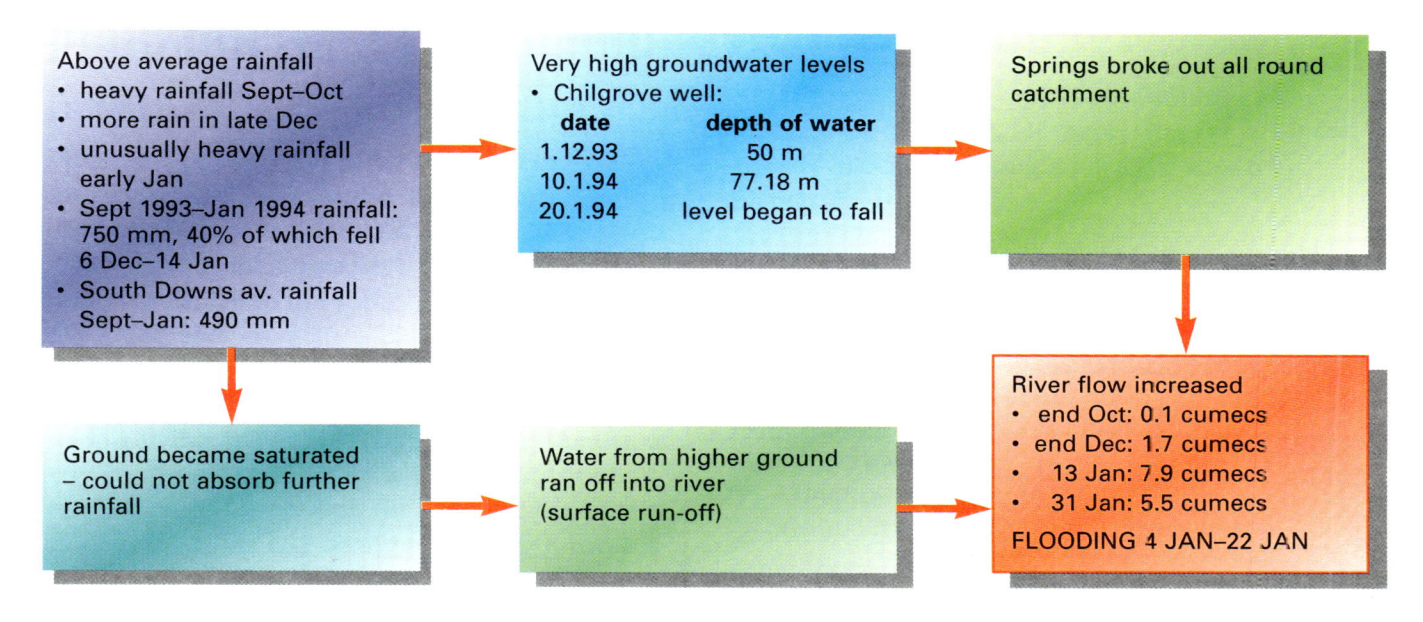

Ground became saturated – could not absorb further rainfall

Figure 9 Effect of above average rainfall

FOUNDATION

Use the information in Figure 9 to answer questions 1 and 2.

1. a) Compare the average amount of September–January rainfall with that for the same period in winter 1993–4. How did the heavy rainfall affect groundwater levels?
   b) Why did this increase the flow of the Lavant?
   c) How else did the heavy rainfall increase the flow of the Lavant?
2. When did flooding first occur in winter 1993–4?
3. a) How much water can the river channel above Chichester carry?
   b) How much water can the culverts under Chichester carry?
   c) Why did flooding occur in Chichester and at Westhampnett Mill?
4. Which parts of the city seem to be flooded most frequently? (See Fig. 5)

The newspaper clips (p.121) will help you to answer questions 5 and 6.

5. List the main problems which flooding brings.
6. List four ways in which these problems were tackled.

HIGHER

1. Describe the sequence of events which led to the flooding in early January 1994.
2. a) What was the principal natural cause of flooding in January 1994?
   b) Which human factor contributed to flooding in Chichester?
   c) What appears to have been the cause in the past? (See Fig. 5)
3. Explain why, following the 1994 flood event, it was decided to improve flood protection not only for Chichester but for the whole of the Lavant valley. (See Fig. 8)

The problem

Two small culverts and a narrow channel convey the Lavant through Chichester and can only cope with a flow not exceeding 4 cumecs. Hence the need to divert excess flow either around or under Chichester.

Decision Making Exercises

Assessing the options for flood alleviation

Any scheme must aim:
- to reduce the risk of flooding to people and property in Chichester
- not to increase the risk of flooding to people and property elsewhere
- to be technically, environmentally and economically acceptable.

Although significant flooding is likely to occur on average every 20 years, flooding of the magnitude of the 1994 flood event would occur probably only once in 100 years or more. This factor must be taken into account when assessing the total cost/benefit factor. If no action is taken then flood damages amounting to £37 million will be incurred over a period of 50 years.

Flood damages for 1994 totalled £5 935 000	
• direct damages	£1 988 000
• business losses (loss of income)	£ 620 000
• West Sussex CC costs for emergency works	£1 905 000
• NRA costs for emergency works	£ 350 000
• road closure costs	£1 072 000

Three viable options were shortlisted which would allow a flow of 8 cumecs to be carried past Chichester.

1 Diversion to Pagham Rife
Flood relief channel from the Lavant at Westhampnett Mill via the Forebridge Rife and Pagham Rife to the sea at Pagham Harbour

2 Diversion to Chichester Canal
Flood relief channel from the Lavant at Westhampnett Mill via the Forebridge Rife, the lakes at Southern Lakeside Village, and Chichester Canal to the sea at Chichester Harbour.

3 Diversion to a tunnel under Chichester
Flood relief channel from the Lavant at Westhampnett Mill via a tunnel under Chichester to rejoin the Lavant south of the A27 Chichester bypass and discharge into Fishbourne Channel.

These options and the location of photographs A and B are shown in Figure 10.

Photo A Option 1: Pagham Rife a few metres above its outfall into Pagham Harbour. Notice the wide, flat floodplain. The South Downs are in the background.

Photo B Option 2: Chichester Canal at Hunston Bridge. The canal is important for its recreation value. The towpath is used by walkers.

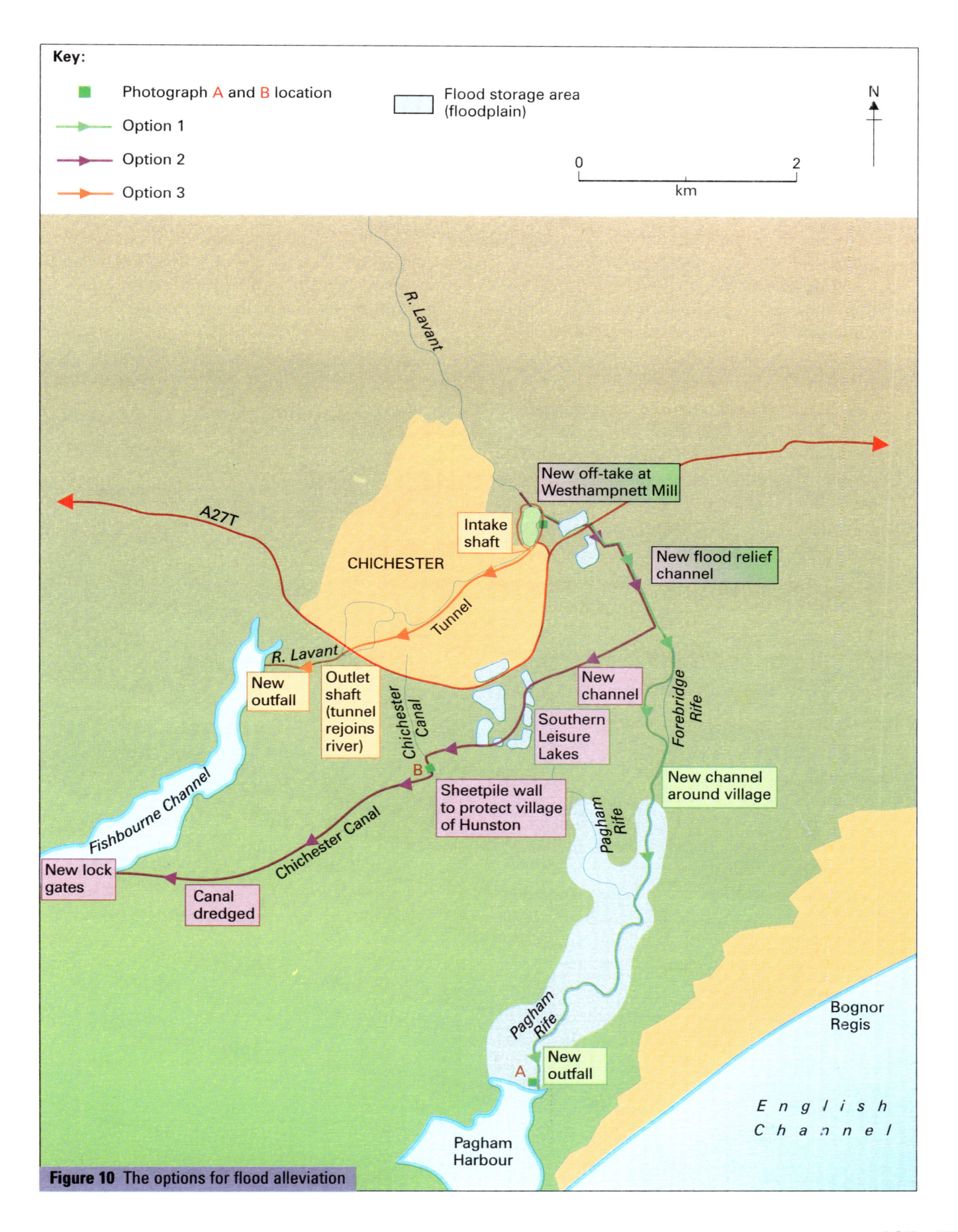

Flood alleviation in the Lavant Valley, Chichester

Figure 10 The options for flood alleviation

125

Decision Making Exercises

Option 1 – Diversion to Pagham Rife

- floodwaters will take a natural route to the sea; this scheme makes use of the Pagham Rife floodplain for storage (R. Lavant originally flowed south from Westhampnett, possibly to the Pagham Rife)
- technically the most straightforward surface scheme, will involve:
  • a section of new channel
  • improvements to sections of existing channel
  • some new flood defence embankments (1 m high)
  • a new outfall at Pagham Harbour
- minimal adverse effect on the environment:
  • agricultural land which will be flooded is already affected by floods when the weather conditions are severe
  • very little property will be affected
- opportunities for increasing the recreational value of the Rife
- cost: £5.4 million; the risks of costs increasing are smaller than in the other two options.

Option 2 – Diversion to the Chichester Canal

- improvement to the canal to carry floodwater to sea
- technically will involve:
  • some bridges for access to agricultural land
  • weirs and sluices to take diverted floodwaters so that they do not affect the use of the lakes for recreational purposes
  • new controls at the locks to reduce the effect of floodwater on water levels, which will affect houseboats moored upstream from the lock
  • protection for the village of Hunston
- will have a significant impact on the environment, for example destruction of reedbeds by the canal, but there would also be opportunities for improvements to the environment such as increased recreational use of the canal
- cost: £7.0 million.

Option 3 – Diversion to tunnel under Chichester

- technically will involve:
  • 2710 m tunnel at depth of 11 m to 17 m to avoid services (e.g. water) and foundations
  • inlet and outlet shafts
  • improvements to existing channel downstream from Chichester
- environmental impact will be minimal but on the other hand there will be no chance for any improvements to the environment:
- impact will be limited to the sites of the inlet and outlet shafts
- in the case of the inlet shaft this would mean a control structure to divert the floodwater into the tunnel
- at the top of the outlet shaft a spillway would be necessary to discharge the floodwater into the improved river channel
- cost: £8.6 million; high risk of cost increases owing to unforeseen ground conditions which may be encountered.

Flood alleviation in the Lavant Valley, Chicheste.

The Decision

FOUNDATION

1. Give three reasons why a scheme to help to reduce the risk of flooding is necessary.
2. For each option state
   a) a way in which the environment will be damaged
   b) whether or not there will be technical problems to cope with during construction
   c) the cost of the scheme.
3. Which scheme a) has least adverse effect on the environment, b) is technically most straightforward, c) is cheapest?
4. Now decide which option you think is the best.

HIGHER

1. Explain, giving as many reasons as possible, why a flood alleviation scheme is necessary.
2. Why is the term 'alleviation' rather than 'prevention' used?
3. Which scheme do you think should be adopted? Give your reasons.

Summary

The 1994 flood event was exceptional. It was the result of a prolonged period of heavy rainfall and high groundwater levels. An intense storm on 30 December 1993 led to surface run-off. Flows in the River Lavant reached nearly twice their previously recorded maximum flow. The Lavant burst its banks in the upper catchment. Floodwaters quickly moved down the Lavant valley to Chichester where the river was confined in two culverts. The capacity of each of these was well below the volume of the swollen river. Extensive flooding occurred in Chichester and the surrounding area to the east and south-east, and in the upper Lavant valley. So serious was the flooding that an evacuation plan was drawn up for the south-east section of the city in case the culvert failed. Flooding lasted for 18 days and caused damages estimated at around £6 million. Clearly, action must be taken if serious flooding is to be avoided. Damages of the order of £37 million will be incurred over a period of 50 years if no action is taken.

Glossary

aquifer water bearing rock

catchment area on which rain falls and feeds into river

culvert underground channel

cumecs cubic metres per second

discharge the amount of water passing through any cross section of a stream in a given time; usually measured in cumecs

permeable allowing water to pass through

1:50 000 maps

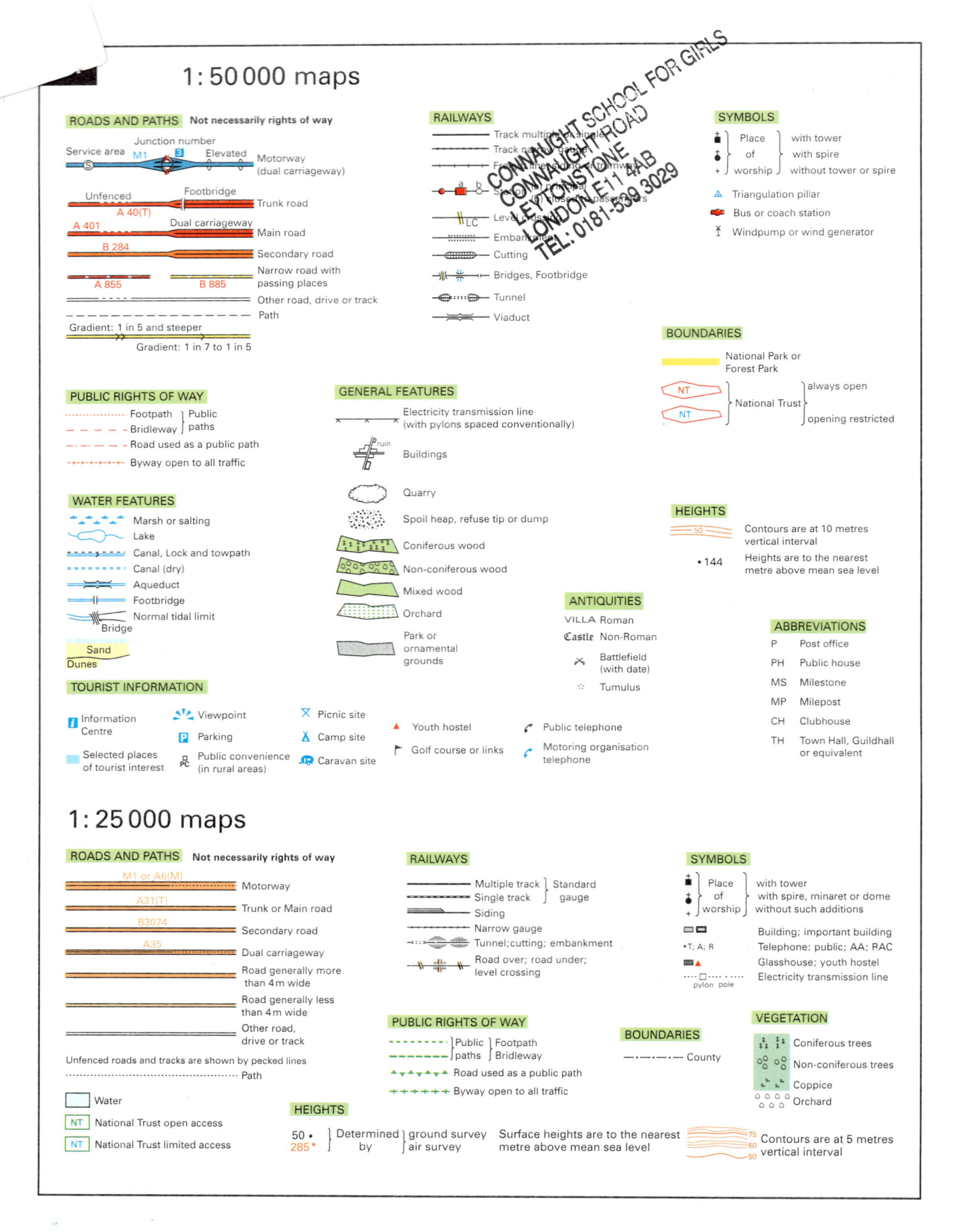

ROADS AND PATHS — Not necessarily rights of way

- Motorway (dual carriageway) — Service area, Junction number, Elevated (M1)
- Trunk road — A 40(T), Unfenced, Footbridge
- Main road — A 401, Dual carriageway
- Secondary road — B 284
- Narrow road with passing places — A 855, B 885
- Other road, drive or track
- Path
- Gradient: 1 in 5 and steeper
- Gradient: 1 in 7 to 1 in 5

PUBLIC RIGHTS OF WAY

- Footpath } Public paths
- Bridleway
- Road used as a public path
- Byway open to all traffic

WATER FEATURES

- Marsh or salting
- Lake
- Canal, Lock and towpath
- Canal (dry)
- Aqueduct
- Footbridge
- Normal tidal limit
- Bridge
- Sand
- Dunes

TOURIST INFORMATION

- Information Centre
- Viewpoint
- Picnic site
- Parking
- Camp site
- Youth hostel
- Public telephone
- Selected places of tourist interest
- Public convenience (in rural areas)
- Caravan site
- Golf course or links
- Motoring organisation telephone

RAILWAYS

- Track multiple or single
- Track narrow gauge
- Freight line, siding or tramway
- Station (a) Main (b) Minor
- Level crossing; passengers — LC
- Embankment
- Cutting
- Bridges, Footbridge
- Tunnel
- Viaduct

GENERAL FEATURES

- Electricity transmission line (with pylons spaced conventionally)
- Buildings (ruin)
- Quarry
- Spoil heap, refuse tip or dump
- Coniferous wood
- Non-coniferous wood
- Mixed wood
- Orchard
- Park or ornamental grounds

ANTIQUITIES

- VILLA — Roman
- Castle — Non-Roman
- Battlefield (with date)
- Tumulus

SYMBOLS

- Place of worship — with tower / with spire / without tower or spire
- Triangulation pillar
- Bus or coach station
- Windpump or wind generator

BOUNDARIES

- National Park or Forest Park
- NT — National Trust, always open
- NT — National Trust, opening restricted

HEIGHTS

- 50 — Contours are at 10 metres vertical interval
- •144 — Heights are to the nearest metre above mean sea level

ABBREVIATIONS

P	Post office
PH	Public house
MS	Milestone
MP	Milepost
CH	Clubhouse
TH	Town Hall, Guildhall or equivalent

1:25 000 maps

ROADS AND PATHS — Not necessarily rights of way

- Motorway — M1 or A6(M)
- Trunk or Main road — A31(T)
- Secondary road — B3074
- Dual carriageway — A35
- Road generally more than 4m wide
- Road generally less than 4m wide
- Other road, drive or track
- Unfenced roads and tracks are shown by pecked lines
- Path
- Water
- NT — National Trust open access
- NT — National Trust limited access

RAILWAYS

- Multiple track } Standard gauge
- Single track
- Siding
- Narrow gauge
- Tunnel; cutting; embankment
- Road over; road under; level crossing

PUBLIC RIGHTS OF WAY

- Public paths } Footpath / Bridleway
- Road used as a public path
- Byway open to all traffic

HEIGHTS

- 50• ground survey } Determined by
- 285• air survey
- Surface heights are to the nearest metre above mean sea level

SYMBOLS

- Place of worship — with tower / with spire, minaret or dome / without such additions
- Building; important building
- •T; A; R — Telephone: public; AA; RAC
- Glasshouse; youth hostel
- Electricity transmission line — pylon, pole

BOUNDARIES

- County

VEGETATION

- Coniferous trees
- Non-coniferous trees
- Coppice
- Orchard
- Contours are at 5 metres vertical interval (75, 60, 50)

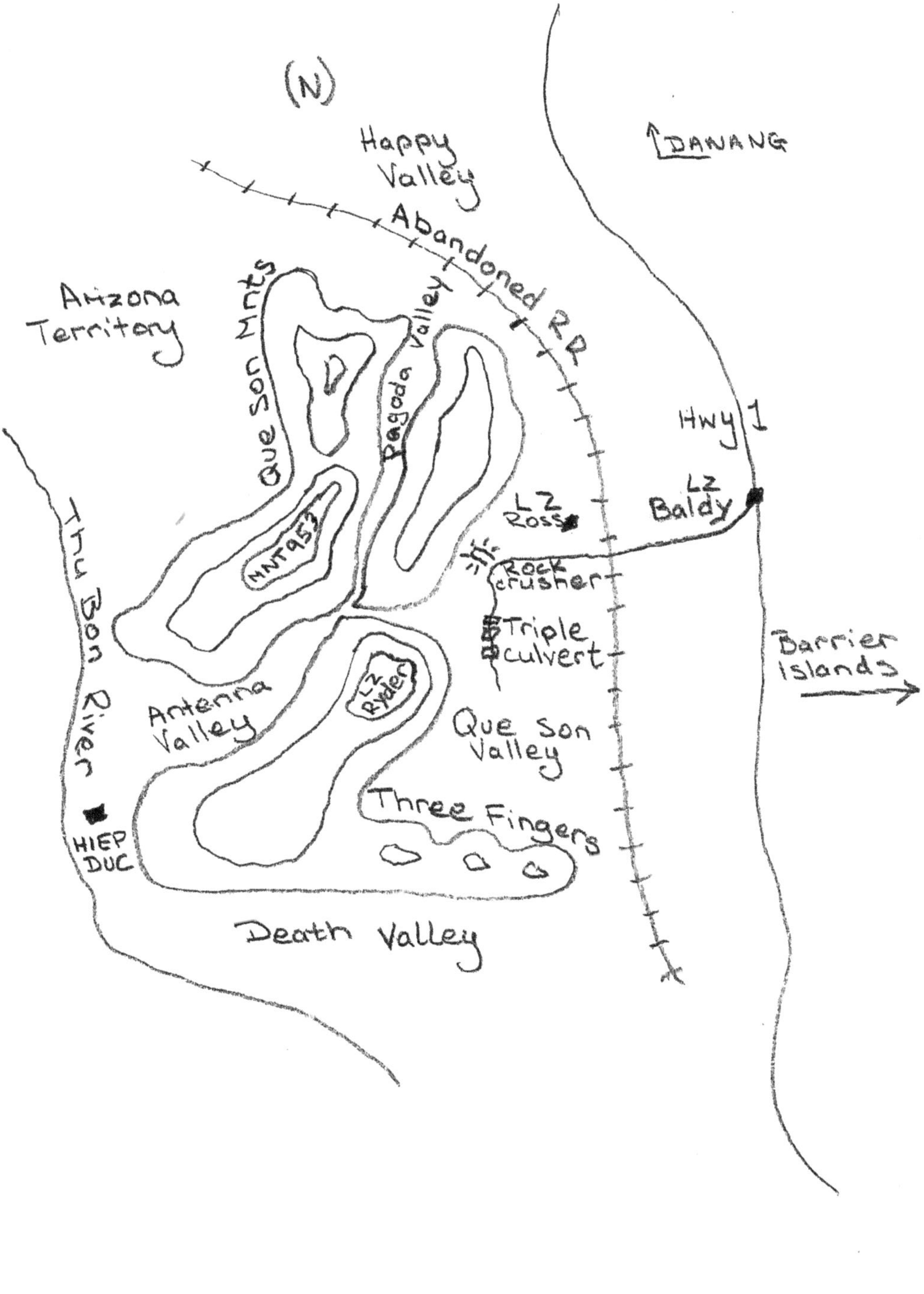
(N)
DANANG
Happy Valley
Abandoned RR
Arizona Territory
Que Son Mnts
Pagoda Valley
Hwy 1
LZ Baldy
LZ Ross
Rock crusher
Triple culvert
Barrier Islands
MNT953
Thu Bon River
Antenna Valley
LZ Ryder
Que Son Valley
Three Fingers
HIEP DUC
Death Valley